These recipes and kitchen tricks make hosting so fun and effortless that you can actually enjoy the party. And solo snack dinners have never looked so good.

For fans of cheese boards, charcuterie, tinned seafood, and snack-focused meals, *Party Tricks* embraces the way we want to cook and eat today, swapping the rigidity of a formal dinner party in favor of casual, carefree assemblages of small plates packed with big flavor. Who needs to serve a meat, a starch, and a vegetable when you can offer an array of simple, sophisticated snacks that come together at a moment's notice and taste exceptional?

Here, *Tin to Table* author Anna Hezel leans into the luxury of fancy snacky food via 50 recipes that draw inspiration from glamorous bar nibbles and retro classics:

— MAPLE BUTTER SHICHIMI TOGARASHI POPCORN

— SALT & VINEGAR CHIPS WITH CRÈME FRAÎCHE & TROUT ROE

— WHIPPED FETA WITH BURNT HONEY

— CONFITED CHERRY TOMATOES

— SHRIMP BUTTER & CUCUMBER SANDWICHES ON BRIOCHE

— PISTACHIO MAGIC SHELL

— SUNGOLD VANILLA SHRUB

Filled with party prep wisdom, from stocking your pantry to building a menu, *Party Tricks* equips you to be the kind of relaxed host who throws regular get-togethers with food so tasty your friends won't stop talking about it—and to be your own best chef for solo dinners. With the right easy, elegant bites, any meal can be a party.

Party Tricks

PARTY *Tricks*

EASY, ELEGANT RECIPES FOR SNACKING AND HOSTING

ANNA HEZEL

Photography by LINDA XIAO • *Illustrations by* CHARLOTTE FARMER

CHRONICLE BOOKS
SAN FRANCISCO

Library of Congress Cataloging-in-Publication Data

Names: Hezel, Anna author | Xiao, Linda photographer | Farmer, Charlotte illustrator
Title: Party tricks : easy, elegant recipes for snacking and hosting / Anna Hezel ; photography by Linda Xiao ; illustrations by Charlotte Farmer.
Description: San Francisco : Chronicle Books, [2026] | Includes index.
Identifiers: LCCN 2025029409 | ISBN 9781797234502 hardcover
Subjects: LCSH: Snack foods | Dinners and dining | Entertaining | LCGFT: Cookbooks
Classification: LCC TX740 .H498 2026 | DDC 641.5/3--dc23/eng/20250707
LC record available at https://lccn.loc.gov/2025029409

Manufactured in China.

Prop styling by Maeve Sheridan.
Food styling by Barrett Washburne.
Designed by Lizzie Vaughan.
Typesetting by Frank Brayton.

10 9 8 7 6 5 4 3 2 1

Chronicle books and gifts are available at special quantity discounts to corporations, professional associations, literacy programs, and other organizations. For details and discount information, please contact our premiums department at corporatesales@chroniclebooks.com or at 1-800-759-0190.

Chronicle Books LLC
680 Second Street
San Francisco, California 94107
www.chroniclebooks.com

For Dorothy

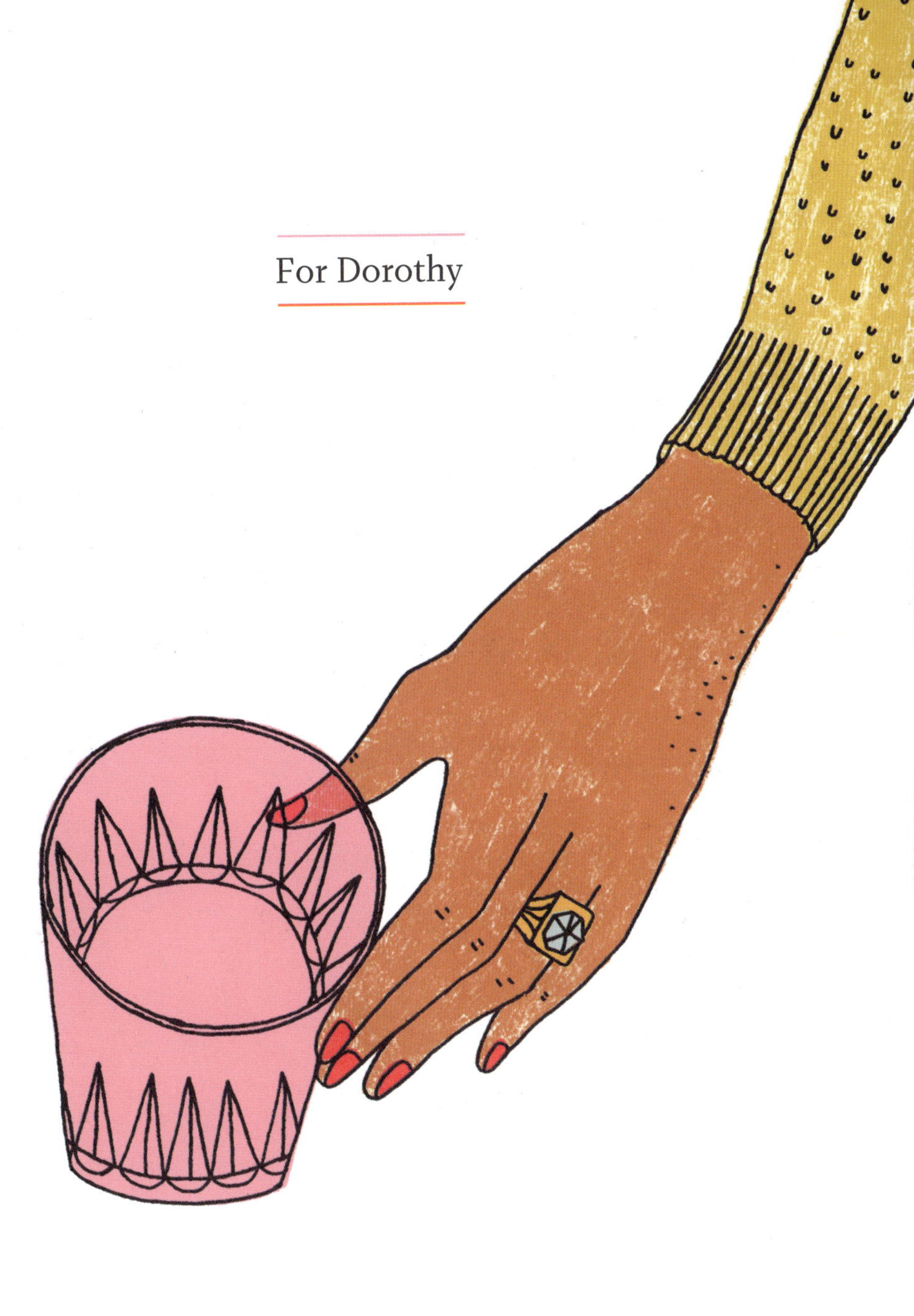

Therry
ZIQUER
ITALIA
Cherry
beer
SARDINES

TABLE OF CONTENTS
You're Invited

SNACKS BEFORE DINNER

PARTY PREP COMPONENTS

Contents

SWEETS

DRINKS

SNACKS FOR DINNER

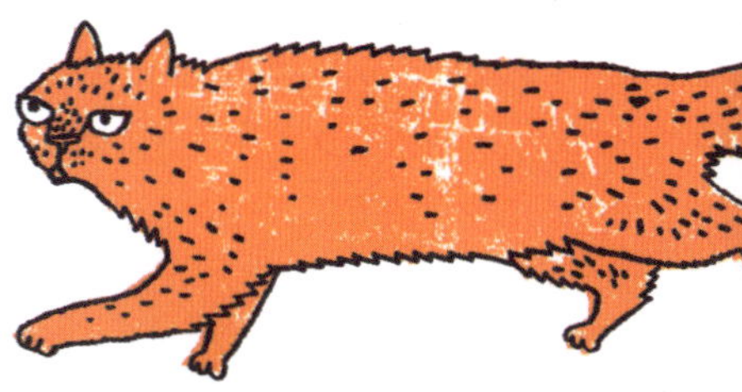

HERO BRAND
SUPERIOR
SARDINES
IN OLIVE OIL

"The cocktail party no longer means a bottle of gin, a can of sardines, and a package of potato chips from the corner grocery," wrote James Beard in his 1940 book, *Hors D'Oeuvre and Canapés*.

When I first read this line a few years ago while editing a group of articles about canapés, I thought to myself, *This hosting faux pas actually sounds like a pretty good party*:

JUST OPEN THE SARDINES, POUR THE CHIPS INTO A NICE BOWL, AND TURN THE BOTTLE OF GIN INTO A ROUND OF MARTINIS.

What's the problem, James?

But Beard was advocating for a more premeditated form of hospitality—one where you might spend a month composing the perfect guest list, another month planning the most impressive menu and shopping for cloth cocktail napkins, and hours carving out wells in homemade pickles to stuff with crab salad.

As a cookbook author, a former editor at publications like *TASTE* and *Epicurious*, and a lifelong party host, I respect this attitude of strategizing and obsessing, and I do love an elaborate project. I spent a lot of hours of my childhood in Buffalo helping my maternal grandmother, Dorothy, craft elaborate seasonal tablescapes and thinking up complicated and architectural desserts to make for gatherings of middle school friends. Sometimes I find myself wistfully paging through Martha Stewart's first book, *Entertaining*, and thinking about Martha as a young caterer in the early '80s, piping Saint André cheese into hundreds of snow peas.

But even the most ambitious, experienced party hosts have to

PICK THEIR BATTLES, PARE DOWN THE PARTY MENU, AND SIMPLIFY THEIR TO-DO LIST FROM TIME TO TIME.

Doing this will make you less stressed out when the party begins. You'll have more time to top up your friends' wineglasses and catch up with them, and you won't accidentally be stingy with the food because you ran out of steam after stuffing the tenth snow pea with cheese.

"The hostess, too, should be able to participate and not have to spend her time in the kitchen cooking, tasting and seasoning," wrote Lois Levine and Marian Burros in the introduction to their now legendary 1960 cookbook *Elegant but Easy*. The pair go on to promise that you can pull this off without hiring help *or* relying completely on premade foods from the grocery store. The ensuing book (which was the origin of the *New York Times*'s famous plum torte) offers clever, semi-homemade solutions to getting three- or four-course meals on the table.

We're long past the era when a home cook needed to serve four courses in order to be a great host. Today's modern cook is more likely to have a favorite brand of anchovies or a favorite bottle of vinegar on their countertop (that they use on *everything*) than to have their grandmother's best pot roast recipe memorized. Who needs to serve a meat, a starch, and a vegetable at parties when you can craft an array of casual bites that emphasize great ingredients and simple techniques? As James Beard pointed out,

> "HORS D'OEUVRE ARE THE MOST ELASTIC OF FOODS, FOR THEY MAY FIT INTO ANY FORM AND SERVICE."

At a time when we've never had better access to a comprehensive variety of pantry ingredients, this attitude isn't just changing the way we host—it's also changing the way we eat out at restaurants and during restorative nights at home. And why not bring a sense of celebration and variety to weeknight dinners? We're abandoning the rigidity of long recipes in favor of fun, carefree assemblages of snacks with big flavor packed into every bite.

I have noticed my own everyday eating habits moving in this direction, especially after writing my previous cookbook,

Tin to Table, which gave me a professional excuse to amass an ungodly collection of tinned seafood from around the world. A lot of my weekday desk lunches at home look like I just snuck out for a moment to hit a cocktail party buffet—a few pieces of toasted bread, a smattering of raw veggies, a bit of cherry tomato confit, some sardines, a handful of olives.

The recipes in this book lean into the luxury and ease of this style of cooking and eating, playing up iconic flavor combinations that don't require a ton of fussing (or a lengthy ingredient list) to taste good.

Drawing inspiration from glamorous bar snacks, retro classics, and nostalgic childhood foods,

THESE RECIPES WILL TURN YOUR KITCHEN COUNTER INTO THE BEST WINE BAR IN TOWN, WHETHER YOU'RE COOKING FOR YOURSELF OR TWENTY OF YOUR BEST FRIENDS.

THE PARTY PANTRY

While you might find yourself busily running around the day of a party to pick up cheese or flowers, a lot of the crucial ingredients for hosting are things you'll want to keep in your pantry at all times. Keeping these ingredients around will mean that you're extra ready for thirty-person cocktail parties. But it will also mean that you can quickly piece together lazy, snack-focused dinners on weeknights when the idea of even boiling pasta water feels like an affront, or whip up a quick bite to eat if someone stops by and stays for a whole bottle of wine. These are some of the essentials that are always worth the pantry space.

TINNED SEAFOOD

Much like a good cheese or piece of charcuterie, tinned seafood is a convenient way to showcase someone else's hard work and preservation techniques, making your job in the kitchen extremely easy. All you really have to do is open a tin and arrange it with some pickles, almonds, crackers—whatever you have around. My last book, *Tin to Table*, has loads of advice about how to start a collection of tinned seafood and cook with it and serve it, but at a minimum, I think everyone should have some sardines packed in olive oil, mussels in escabeche sauce, and cured anchovies packed in olive oil.

These three items are all low on the food chain, making them some of the more sustainable options available. These are all party-ready without any fussing or cooking, but they'll also allow you to make recipes like the Piparra Sardine Butter (page 50), Pickled Mussel Gildas (page 91), and Matrimonio Tartine (page 131).

Even though I think of tinned anchovies as a pantry ingredient, I keep mine in the fridge since they're a semi-preserved product that can degrade in quality over time at warm temperatures.

BRINY THINGS IN JARS

Open my fridge at any given time, and you will find a gallery of pickled impulse purchases—the cocktail onions I bought during a Gibson craving, the caper berries I picked up for a fancy salad, and the pickled okra I thought might count as a "side dish" to have with smashburgers. I don't regret any of them, because pickles go with everything. They can fill out relish trays, garnish canapés, or add a satisfying crunch to spreads and dips.

To start your stash, I recommend cornichons, which are an essential accompaniment to the Cheese Dreams (page 109); piparras, a spicy pickled Spanish pepper that tastes great with tinned fish; and some olives, which can work as an immediate snack to set out while you're frying the last few Canned Clam Croquettes (page 115) or putting the final touches on your Whipped Feta with Burnt Honey (page 97).

CHIPS AND CRACKERS

You could have a very fun night in with a bottle of Cava, a bag of chips, and a tin of mussels. But when you're hosting a party, the more crunchy carbs, the better. Saltines and Ritz crackers bring a retro factor and are perfect for spreading with Shrimp Butter (page 123) or Piparra Sardine Butter (page 50). Pretzels are classic alongside Apples & Gouda Drizzled with Honey & Black Pepper (page 83) or in Rosemary Brown Sugar Party Mix (page 64).

A FEW GOOD OLIVE OILS

I'm a strong believer in a two-bottle olive oil system. At any given time, I have a gigantic bottle of a not-too-expensive, mild-tasting option, which I use for cooking tasks like emulsifying a Caesar Aioli (page 53), making Confited Cherry Tomatoes (page 99), or frying Canned Clam Croquettes (page 115). I like to complement this pantry staple with a smaller bottle of a fresh, grassy, peppery olive oil that's ideal for drizzling over finished dishes (like the Whipped Feta with Burnt Honey on page 97).

A FEW GOOD SALTS

If you haven't already guessed from all the talk of anchovies and potato chips, this is a very salty cookbook (even the desserts are pretty salty). An almost idiotic amount of space in my spice drawer is dedicated to salt in various shapes, sizes, colors, and crystal structures. But if I had to scrap it all and start my salt collection over again, I'd focus on a box of kosher salt (for most cooking) and a box of large flaky salt (for when you really want a *crunch*). For recipes in this book that call for kosher salt, I recommend using Diamond Crystal, which is less salty per volume than other brands. This gives you more control, so that extra ⅛ of a teaspoon you accidentally spill into a batch of cookies won't push it over the edge toward unbearable saltiness.

NUTS

Much like that jar of olives, a bag of nuts will come in handy when you need one more thing to set out for guests to snack on while you finish the more involved dishes. While I'm not the biggest fan of mixed nuts (each one cooks in a different amount of time, so you always end up with a few that are burnt and a few that are sad and chewy), I like keeping a variety of pistachios, pecans, almonds, and hazelnuts around. These will be crucial for making Candied Marcona Almonds (page 76), Rosemary Brown Sugar Party Mix (page 64), and Ham & Hazelnuts (page 67), and the leftover odds and ends can be blended into pesto or toasted and crushed to sprinkle on oatmeal.

Although nuts might seem like any other shelf-stable baking ingredient or pantry staple, it's important to remember that they're an agricultural product with a shelf life. If they've been sitting in a cupboard for too long, they can get stale, and the oils inside them can go rancid. For the freshest flavor and crunchiest texture, use these up and replace them often (that means that the half bag of pecans you have left over in your baking drawer from last Thanksgiving has got to go). If you're storing nuts for longer than a couple months, move them to an airtight container in your freezer.

CHOCOLATE

A small reserve of good chocolate opens up opportunities for weekend baking projects and late-night batches of Lightning-Fast Chocolate Pudding (page 150). For desserts, I like to stick with dark chocolate bars or disks with cacao percentages of around 60% to 70%. In this range, the chocolate melts beautifully and its flavor isn't diluted by too much sugar. If your kitchen runs warm, you can try a trick I learned a few years ago from chocolatier Jacques Torres and store your chocolate inside a ziplock bag in the freezer. To avoid condensation forming on the chocolate's surface, just make sure the chocolate has warmed to room temperature before opening the sealed bag.

Even if you don't have time for a baking project, as long as you have some quality chocolate around, you can put together a phoned-in (but still classy) dessert plate. Just break a few chocolate bars into shards and arrange them on a plate with some clementines or other fresh fruit, and pour a round of amaros.

SELTZER

Having a good supply of bubbly water is crucial for party preparedness. I'm lucky enough to get my seltzer each month from Brooklyn Seltzer Boys, a company that's been hand-delivering their glass siphon bottles to New York homes and businesses for more than seventy years. Their motto, "Good seltzer should hurt," speaks to their dedication to aggressive carbonation, and it explains why I think theirs is the best for highballs, spritzes, and egg creams.

Even if you don't have the extremely Brooklyn amenity of a seltzer delivery service, you can stock up on this staple so that you're ready to stay hydrated between sips of wine, mix a drink with Sungold Vanilla Shrub (page 182), or make a Punt e Mes & Soda (page 175) or Mini Sour Cherry Ice Cream Float (page 163).

THE PARTY GEAR

While I'd love to have a walk-in pantry full of catering supplies, what I have instead is a few crowded kitchen shelves, augmented by a couple of boxes of backup plates and tea lights shoved into the cob-webbed upper corners of a coat closet. Living in a tight space may limit how many cake stands you can collect, but it doesn't have to prevent you from hosting friends with generosity and great cocktail glasses. I like to think that the limitations have made me even more discerning about which tools and supplies are really necessary, and more creative about getting my use out of them. Here are a few items I think any host should own in order to be ready for a party at a moment's notice.

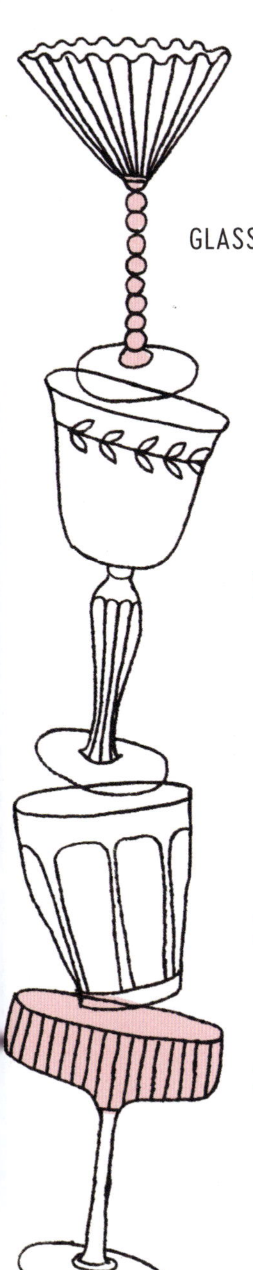

GLASSWARE (MADE OF ACTUAL GLASS)

Of course, there are times when plastic cups just make sense (like a toddler's birthday party or a picnic for five hundred people), but in most cases, I think it's worth the extra dishwashing effort to use real glasses. I feel so strongly about this that I personally hand-washed seventy vintage champagne coupes the night before my own wedding. Let me make my case.

1 They're inexpensive and infinitely reusable. I've picked up sets of glasses from restaurant wholesale suppliers, flea markets, and even for free on the sidewalk. If you keep an eye on thrift store selections and your local Buy Nothing groups, you can put together an inexpensive selection that will last you for years, which beats routinely spending money on cups that will end up in the garbage after an hour or two of use.

2 It's okay if one breaks. Turn on the overhead light for a minute and vacuum the pieces up. That's one less glass you have to wash and put away later.

3 Drinking out of a glass just feels better. Whether you're drinking a really nice bottle of wine or a dive bar cocktail, everything tastes better out of a glass. And glass is more pleasant to hold than a squeaky plastic cup.

While I'm not particular about having the "right" glass for every style of wine, spirit, or cocktail, I find that a dozen each of stemmed coupes (for sparkling wine or cocktails served straight up) and stackable bodega glasses (for non-sparkling wine or drinks with ice) usually covers my bases. Either style can easily double as a serving dish for desserts like Fireplace Gelato (page 145), Salty Peanut Butter Budino with Toffee-Toasted Cornflakes (page 154), and Lightning-Fast Chocolate Pudding (page 150).

COCKTAIL PICKS

If you're going to be eccentric about one party-hosting accessory, make it cocktail picks, which take up very little room in a drawer but save you from having to serve everything with cutlery. You can buy these in any number of colors and styles (with Christmas trees, or skulls, or baseballs at the ends) from restaurant supply wholesalers like webstaurantstore.com or pickonus.com, and websites like eBay and Etsy are full of reusable stainless-steel sets. I like to always have some 4½ in [11 cm] picks handy to use for cocktail garnishes or pintxos, plus a few shorter ones (around 3½ in [9 cm]) to use for skewering one-bite snacks.

NAPKINS

I love to use linen for sit-down dinner parties when I know no one will set down their napkin somewhere in the room and lose track of it. But for any gathering that's larger, I like the practicality of having a few stacks of 5 in [13 cm] square paper cocktail napkins stationed around the room that can double as drink coasters. I like to order these online in large quantities, in solid colors that I know I won't get sick of so that I don't end up with a million half-used packages crammed into a drawer.

CANDLES

To light up a room in a soft, atmospheric way, turn off any overhead lights, turn on a few lamps, and light some unscented candles. With a pack of tea lights from the dollar store, any cocktail glass, empty jar, or small bowl can become a votive. If you're looking for candles that will have a little more longevity (some tea lights will burn out after three or four hours), Ikea sells 3¼ in [8 cm] block candles that burn for up to 15 hours.

A FEW CHEAP PITCHERS

For ice water and various nonalcoholic offerings (like the Mint & Maple Iced Tea on page 181), you'll want to have a few large pitchers on hand. I'm a fan of glass half-gallon [1.9 L] pitchers with plastic lids. The lid will keep fridge smells out of the pitcher when you're storing it but can be removed when it's time to pour drinks.

A FEW PLATTER-SHAPED THINGS

While you'll need a few serving vessels to throw a party, they don't necessarily have to be platters. Smaller bites (like the Pickled Mussel Gildas on page 91) can fit in a kaleidoscope pattern on a dinner plate or nestled into a shallow bowl. To avoid having a big stack of heavy, single-use dishes in the back of the cabinet, put together a collection of wooden cutting boards, enameled baking dishes (I love serving food out of my Dansk Købenstyle casserole dishes), and vintage melamine trays to hold snacks.

ONE REALLY BIG MIXING BOWL THAT CAN DOUBLE AS AN ICE BUCKET

A 5 or 6 quart [4.7 or 5.7 L] metal mixing bowl is useful for tossing salads, letting bread dough rise, and making giant batches of Rosemary Brown Sugar Party Mix (page 64). But its real powers come into play when it's time to chill drinks. Use this bowl to cool down room-temperature wine extra fast (see page 177 for instructions) or to keep open bottles cold without having to make constant trips to and from the refrigerator. If you want to put out ice for guests to add to their beverages, use a separate, smaller bowl with a scoop (no one wants to drink a cocktail made with ice that's touched the outsides of all those dusty bottles).

SERVING UTENSILS WITH CHARACTER

They don't have to match. Like cocktail picks, serving utensils take up very little room in a drawer but are extremely useful. I keep around a mish-mash of Bakelite-handled cake knives, vintage butter and cheese knives, sardine forks (with tines curved perfectly for scooping up a meaty sardine), and ornate serving spoons so that I always have the right tool for the job.

BUILD YOUR PERFECT PARTY MENU

For me, the inspiration for a party menu can begin with a really fruitful grocery shopping trip, a particular recipe I'm dying to try, or a seasonal ingredient I want to celebrate. Even when the first flicker of an idea comes easily, figuring out the rest of the menu can often be the hard part. While there's nothing stopping you from flipping through this book (and the rest of your cookbook library) and dog-earing everything that catches your eye, here are a few pieces of advice I like to follow when creating a party menu.

Whether your party starts at 6:00 p.m. or 9:00 p.m., you can count on at least a few people showing up with dinner-sized hunger.

Plan on a mix of lighter snacks and heartier bites, assuming that each guest will eat about one serving of everything you make. If you're getting nervous about quantities the day of the party, buy a few extra loaves of bread and open a few extra tins of sardines.

Design your menu with a mix of make-ahead items and recipes that require day-of attention.

If I have friends coming over in an hour, I really don't want to be slowly drizzling olive oil into a bowl of egg yolks and whisking them into an aioli. I want to be setting candles out, getting the music volume right, and pouring myself a glass of wine. That's why I like to create a list of the recipes (or discrete tasks) I can finish a day or two ahead of time. This buys me some day-of time to relax, have fun, and actually talk to the people I have invited over.

To keep things from getting boring, think about your party menu in courses, even if it's a casual cocktail party with no plates or cutlery.

Try to come up with a menu that's varied in terms of appearance, texture, flavor, and temperature. The ideal mix will have some fresh ingredients, some cooked elements, some things that are cold and crunchy, and some that are warm and toasty. You want to make sure that the first people in the door have a few small things to nibble on while they're sipping their first drink, but you also want to roll out nice surprises throughout the night—a skillet of Confited Cherry Tomatoes (page 99) or Shrimp in Chili-Garlic Browned Butter (page 125) just as people are getting tired of gnawing on crudités, or a plate of warm Freezer Reserve Pistachio-Sesame Chocolate Chip Cookies (page 159) when your friends are getting tired of savory snacks altogether.

A PARTY PREP TIMELINE

In the interest of making your party run smoothly (and keeping you prepared with snack supplies when the mood strikes), here are some of the recipes you can get a head start on in the days and weeks before your party. If you're too busy in the days before, or you're having a spontaneous gathering (sometimes the urge to entertain just sneaks up on you), don't worry—I have you covered too.

WHAT TO MAKE A FEW WEEKS BEFORE

The CANNED CLAM CROQUETTES (PAGE 115) require a few minutes of frying before serving, but you can do everything else (making the filling, forming it into logs, and breading those logs) ahead of time and keep these in the freezer until then.

You can make the CHEESE DREAMS (PAGE 109) entirely ahead of time and pop them straight from the freezer into a 400°F [200°C] oven for a snack that will beat anything from the hors d'oeuvre section of the freezer aisle.

Make a batch of the SUNGOLD VANILLA SHRUB (PAGE 182) whenever you can get your hands on good, ripe Sungold tomatoes, and you'll have a month's worth of sparkling cocktails.

You don't need any excuse to keep a batch of FREEZER RESERVE PISTACHIO-SESAME CHOCOLATE CHIP COOKIES (PAGE 159) dough on deck. Freeze the dough balls now and thank yourself later.

WHAT TO MAKE A FEW DAYS BEFORE

Everything in CHAPTER 1: PARTY PREP COMPONENTS (PAGE 43) is designed to be made ahead so that you can add sprinkles of CRUNCHY SEED CONFETTI (PAGE 51) and VANILLA SALT (PAGE 56) to zhuzh up last-minute snacks and desserts.

For a semi-ridiculous snack centerpiece, make a batch of PIPARRA SARDINE BUTTER (PAGE 50) a day or two before your party, and refrigerate it in a fish-shaped copper mold. Pop it out of the mold and cover in radish-slice fish scales right before serving.

You can make the ROSEMARY BROWN SUGAR PARTY MIX (PAGE 64) up to a week in advance (although I like to make it a day or two before serving it for the freshest rosemary flavor) so that it's ready to pour into your cutest glass bowl or candy dish at cocktail hour.

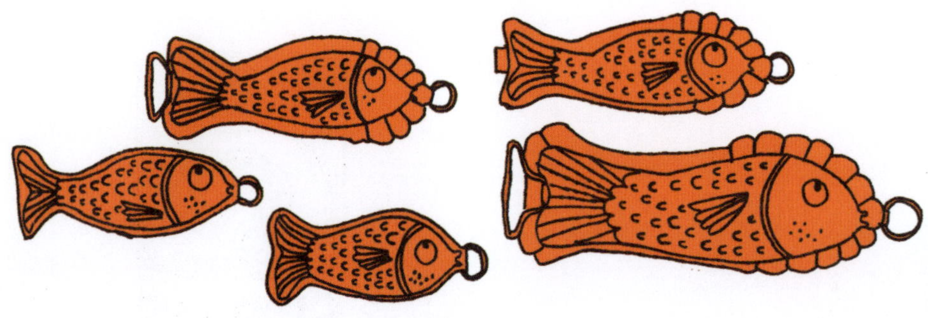

Making the WHIPPED FETA WITH BURNT HONEY (PAGE 97) one or two days ahead gives you time to clean and put away your blender, but it also gives you time to chill the dip so that it's extra creamy and refreshing. You can make the burnt honey ahead of time too—just refrigerate it in a separate small, sealed container.

Once you've whisked together the aioli, you can open a tin whenever the mood strikes over the next couple days, for some TINNED BARNACLES WITH SMOKED PAPRIKA AIOLI (PAGE 89).

Even though the PLUM GRANITA WITH WHIPPED CREAM & CARAMEL SAUCE (PAGE 157) requires some assembly, each of the three components can be made ahead of time and then layered in a coupe glass to serve.

A day's rest in the fridge helps the LIGHTNING-FAST CHOCOLATE PUDDING WITH COCOA CRUNCH (PAGE 150) set, and the topping will stay crunchy in a sealed container on your countertop for several days.

Similar to the chocolate pudding, the SALTY PEANUT BUTTER BUDINO WITH TOFFEE-TOASTED CORNFLAKES (PAGE 154) benefits from a night (or a full day) in the fridge and a (premade) crunchy topping.

WHAT TO MAKE IF YOU PROCRASTINATED YOUR PREP (OR YOU'RE HAVING AN IMPROMPTU PARTY)

Requiring just a few minutes of stovetop hazelnut toasting, the HAM & HAZELNUTS (PAGE 67) is faster to assemble than a full-blown charcuterie board—and it's more interesting.

Don't have time to make a dip? Just assemble the SALT AND VINEGAR CHIPS WITH CRÈME FRAÎCHE & TROUT ROE (PAGE 71).

A warm batch of MAPLE BUTTER SHICHIMI TOGARASHI POPCORN (PAGE 80) is a perfect drinking snack, and it makes your apartment smell amazing.

Refreshing, salty, and satisfying, the PICKLED MUSSEL GILDAS (PAGE 91) can be made entirely from your pantry.

For the CONFITED CHERRY TOMATOES (PAGE 99), all you need to do is dump a few ingredients into a skillet, stick them in the oven, and let time do its thing.

The NECTARINES WITH RICOTTA, OLIVE OIL & BLACK PEPPER (PAGE 119) is less of a recipe and more of a seasonal assemblage of good ingredients.

With only a handful of ingredients and a few minutes of cooking time, the SHRIMP IN CHILI-GARLIC BROWNED BUTTER (PAGE 125) will add a hearty, savory element to your snack spread (with plenty of garlic-tinged butter for bread-soaking).

In late summer and early fall, I find myself adding CANTALOUPE WITH VANILLA SALT (PAGE 147) to menus incessantly.

FIREPLACE GELATO (PAGE 145) has it all. It's a three-ingredient dessert with a touch of caffeine, a hint of amaro, and just the right dose of sweetness.

PISTACHIO MAGIC SHELL (PAGE 165) is a microwave-friendly party trick that works with almost any flavor of ice cream you have knocking around in your freezer. (Chocolate, cherry, and salted caramel are my favorites.)

PUNT E MES & SODA (PAGE 175) is a two-ingredient cocktail that comes together in the glass and has a world of complexity in every sip.

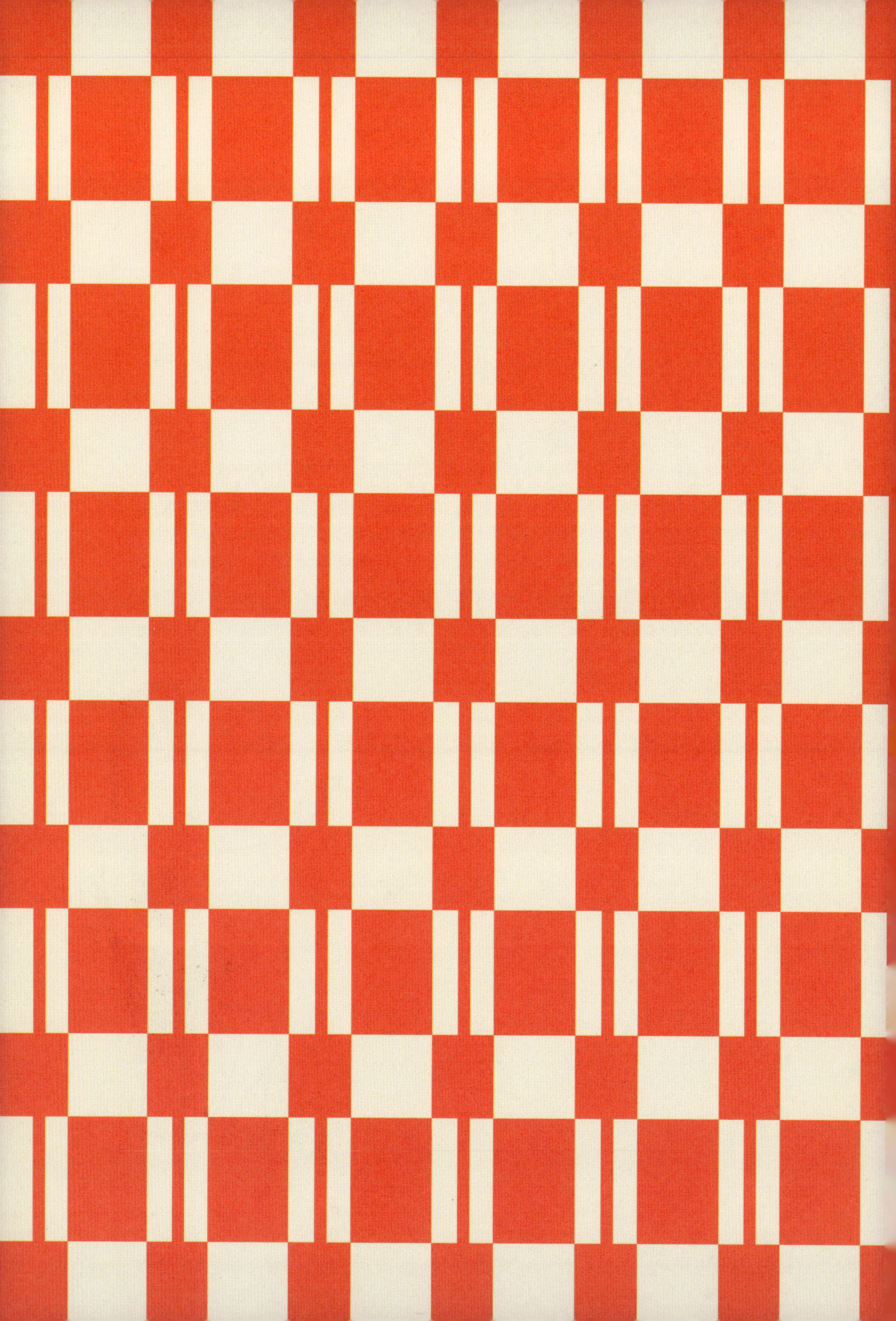

PARTY

Prep

COMPONENTS

MAKE AHEADS • STOCK THE PANTRY

PARTY *Prep* COMPONENTS

As soon as I start planning a party, alongside the many competing Notes app menus and shopping lists, I start a log of which little cooking tasks I can knock out of the way in the week beforehand. Sometimes it's a syrup that will go into a drink, a crunchy topping for a dessert, or a compound butter. Putting this extra bit of legwork into preparing means that I'll be left with fewer dishwasher loads the day of the party and more time to think about a non-awkward way to arrange the chairs in the living room or where to stick that floor lamp for peak ambience.

In this chapter, you'll find some of the components that are worth making ahead of time in generous quantities. That way, you can make the rest of the recipes in this book and be prepared to add bursts of flavor and texture on impulse whenever you're throwing together dinner or improvising a party snack based on what you found at the farmers' market.

There's a Crunchy Seed Confetti **(PAGE 51)** that works on fresh tomatoes, salads, or sprinkled over dips and spreads. You'll find yourself using the Caesar Aioli **(PAGE 53)** as a dip for crudités, a topping for oeufs mayo, and a spread on baguette sandwiches. And whenever your chocolate-filled desserts or fresh fruit are missing a little something, the Vanilla Salt **(PAGE 56)** pulls its weight, showing your guests that you've put thought and care into every fleck-sized detail.

PICKLED CELERY

MAKES ABOUT 1½ CUPS [200 G]

½ CUP [120 ML] DISTILLED VINEGAR
1 TSP KOSHER SALT
1 TSP SUGAR
2 GARLIC CLOVES
1 TSP BLACK PEPPERCORNS
1 CLOVE
¼ TSP CORIANDER SEEDS
4 CELERY STALKS [ABOUT 200 G], CUT INTO 1½ IN [4 CM] LENGTHS

From Victorian celery vases to mid-century relish trays, celery has been part of hosting parties in the United States for many generations. At gatherings hosted by my grandma Dorothy in western New York in the '90s, I remember big stalks of celery resting in pitchers of salt water in the middle of every table, acting as both a palate-cleansing snack and a centerpiece. Similarly, this recipe for pickled celery can function as a garnish (consider skewering it onto a cocktail pick with a cornichon and a cherry tomato for a Bloody Mary), part of a canapé (like the Fried Dates with Blue Cheese & Pickled Celery on page 107), or just as a snack on its own.

DIRECTIONS

In a small saucepan over low heat, combine the vinegar, salt, sugar, garlic, peppercorns, clove, and coriander with ½ cup [120 ml] of water. Cook for about 5 minutes, until the sugar and salt are dissolved. Place the celery in a heatproof bowl, and pour the hot brine over it. Allow the mixture to cool to room temperature, then transfer it to an airtight container. Refrigerate at least overnight before using, and store, refrigerated, for up to 1 week.

MAKES 1¼ CUPS [285 G]

TOMATO CHILI BUTTER

1 CUP [226 G] UNSALTED BUTTER, ROOM TEMPERATURE
¼ CUP [60 G] TOMATO PASTE
1 TSP FINE RED CHILI FLAKES (SUCH AS GOCHUGARU OR PUL BIBER)
½ TSP KOSHER SALT (SEE NOTE)
2 GARLIC CLOVES, FINELY GRATED

With some help from tomato paste and chili flakes, this butter can bring summery warmth to the coldest winter days. It can turn a baguette, salt-cured anchovies, and boquerones into the Matrimonio Tartine (page 131), but it's also dynamic enough to stand out as a spread on hunks of crusty bread or warm cornbread muffins. And the day after the party, you can toss the leftover butter with hot spaghetti and lots of chopped parsley.

DIRECTIONS

In a small saucepan or skillet over medium heat, combine ½ cup [113 g] of the butter with the tomato paste, chili flakes, and salt, whisking frequently. Once the butter is melted, cook for 2 minutes, or until the mixture is bubbly and orange. Remove from the heat, and immediately whisk in the garlic, which will cook from the residual heat.

Add the remaining ½ cup [113 g] of butter, and whisk to combine. Let cool to room temperature, whisking frequently to keep the mixture smooth. Serve immediately, or refrigerate in a sealed container for up to 3 days.

NOTE → If you're making this for the Matrimonio Tartine (page 131), reduce the salt to ¼ tsp since it will be paired with a lot of salty anchovies.

BUTTER

Tricks

THINK OUTSIDE THE STICK

Whether you're making a flavored compound butter or just serving some great cultured butter with bread, give it a retro restaurant flair. Use a small metal Jell-O mold, a silicone chocolate mold, or a wooden butter mold to turn it into seashells, rosettes, fish, or leaves.

TEMPER AND DIP

In the early 2010s, The NoMad took New York by storm with a butter tempering technique that allowed them to serve radishes that looked almost like they had been dipped into an immaculate pot of white chocolate. The technique turned out to be pretty simple. Just melt a stick of butter (½ cup [113 g]) about halfway in the microwave or on the stovetop, and whisk until the butter reaches a uniform consistency that's like melted chocolate. Dip the radishes (with stems left on to give guests something to hold onto) about three-quarters of the way in, and transfer them to a wax paper–lined sheet pan. Sprinkle with salt and refrigerate to chill slightly before serving.

CARVE SOME CURLS

Drag a serrated knife or butter curler across the surface of a stick of cold butter to shave off wavy curls that guests can scoop up and onto their pieces of bread. Set these in a small bowl in the refrigerator until you're ready to serve.

PIPARRA SARDINE BUTTER

MAKES ABOUT 1 CUP [226 G]

½ CUP [113 G] UNSALTED BUTTER, ROOM TEMPERATURE

ONE 4.4 OZ [125 G] TIN OF SARDINES PACKED IN OLIVE OIL, DRAINED

10 PIPARRAS, STEMMED AND MINCED

1 SMALL SHALLOT, MINCED

½ TSP KOSHER SALT

As someone who wrote a book about tinned seafood, I get this question a lot: What's the best way to eat sardines? There's no wrong answer, but I love to enjoy a tin with bread, butter, and a few piparras (pickled guindilla peppers). This silky pâté combines the sardines, butter, and piparras with minced shallot in a form that can be easily spread onto little toasts for a canapé or eaten with a baguette. The easiest way to serve this is in a ramekin on a plate full of saltines, bread, or radishes. But if you want to get creative, pack the butter into a small, fish-shaped copper mold that's been lined with plastic wrap, and refrigerate until you're ready to serve. Decorate the outside of the fish with thin radish slices for scales, some celery leaves or parsley for the tail, and a caper for an eye.

DIRECTIONS

In a small mixing bowl, combine all the ingredients. Use a fork to flake apart the sardines and mix them thoroughly into the butter. Transfer the mixture to a ramekin or a plastic wrap–lined fish mold, cover, and refrigerate until you're ready to serve. This can be made up to 2 days in advance.

MAKES ¼ CUP [35 G]

CRUNCHY SEED CONFETTI

1 TBSP WHITE SESAME SEEDS
1 TBSP BLACK SESAME SEEDS
2 TSP POPPY SEEDS
2 TSP FENNEL SEEDS
2 TSP CARAWAY SEEDS
½ TSP MAPLE SYRUP
¼ TSP OLIVE OIL
¼ TSP KOSHER SALT

Often when I finish making a dip or plating a salad, I feel like it's missing a key textural element: crunch. This is where my handy, versatile seed mix comes in. This sprinkle is a little like an everything bagel seasoning, but with full focus on the seeds (a mix of sesame, poppy, fennel, and caraway). Toasting this seed mix in maple syrup and salt keeps it perfectly seasoned and astoundingly crunchy, even after it's been sitting on top of a swirl of hummus or a plate of juicy tomatoes. Try this sprinkled on the Tomatoes with Chili Butter (page 105), then use the leftover confetti to add texture to bowls of soup, cucumber sandwiches, or scrambled eggs throughout the week.

DIRECTIONS

Preheat the oven to 300°F [150°C].

In the center of a 9 by 13 in [23 by 33 cm] sheet pan, mix all the ingredients together until the oil and maple syrup are evenly distributed. Spread into an even layer. Bake for 15 minutes, stirring the seeds every 5 minutes to prevent any from sticking to the pan and burning.

Remove from the oven and let cool on the pan. Transfer to an airtight container and store at room temperature for up to 1 week.

SMOKED PAPRIKA AIOLI

MAKES ¾ CUP [180 ML]

1 GARLIC CLOVE, GRATED

1 LARGE EGG YOLK

1 TBSP SHERRY VINEGAR

¾ CUP [180 ML] OLIVE OIL

¼ TSP KOSHER SALT

¼ TSP PAPRIKA

¼ TSP SMOKED PAPRIKA, PLUS MORE IF DESIRED

This aioli was originally intended for the Tinned Barnacles with Smoked Paprika Aioli (page 89), but its uses go far beyond one dish. The smoky, slightly garlicky sauce pairs well with other seafood, like tinned mussels or smoked oysters, and you can also try drizzling it over roasted potatoes or spreading it onto a breakfast sandwich. Although making a mayonnaise at home can be intimidating, it's really just a matter of whisking thoroughly while slowly drizzling in the olive oil.

DIRECTIONS

In a small mixing bowl, whisk together the garlic, egg yolk, and vinegar. Very slowly, over the course of several minutes, drizzle the olive oil into the mixing bowl while whisking vigorously. After a few minutes, you should start to see the mixture thicken, eventually reaching a spreadable consistency. If your emulsion breaks (you'll know because it will take on a grainy appearance and become more pourable than it is spreadable), don't panic. Add a new egg yolk to a clean bowl and slowly drizzle in your broken aioli while whisking furiously.

Stir in the salt and both paprikas, adding more smoked paprika, if desired. Store in a sealed container in the refrigerator for up to 3 days.

MAKES 2 CUPS [475 ML]

CAESAR AIOLI

2 GARLIC CLOVES, FINELY GRATED OR MINCED
8 OIL-PACKED ANCHOVY FILLETS, MINCED
2 LARGE EGG YOLKS
2 TBSP DIJON MUSTARD
2 TBSP WHITE WINE VINEGAR
1½ CUPS [360 ML] OLIVE OIL
⅔ CUP [60 G] FINELY GRATED PARMESAN
1 TSP WORCESTERSHIRE SAUCE
¼ TSP BLACK PEPPER, PLUS MORE FOR SERVING

In Provence, a "grand aioli" is a celebratory meal consisting of a rainbow of raw or blanched vegetables and a bracingly garlicky batch of rich aioli to gently coat them. As an anchovy fanatic and a strong believer that Caesar dressing shouldn't be limited to salads, I serve my crudités with a Caesar-ified aioli that's souped up with some garlic, anchovies, Dijon, and Parmesan. Use this for the Caesar Oeufs Mayonnaise with Chicories (page 121) or serve it with a generous platter of crunchy vegetables.

DIRECTIONS

Add the garlic, anchovies, yolks, mustard, and vinegar to a blender or medium mixing bowl. With the blender running (or while whisking vigorously using a metal whisk), start to pour the olive oil into the mix very slowly. Only add a few drops at a time, allowing each addition to be fully incorporated by the blender or whisk. By the time you've added about a cup of the oil, you should notice the mixture start to thicken and lighten in color.

Once all the oil is incorporated, add the remaining ingredients, whisking or blending for a few seconds, until just combined.

Transfer the dip to an airtight container and chill for up to 3 days. To serve, transfer the aioli to a small bowl, and garnish with black pepper.

BEET GOAT CHEESE

MAKES 1½ CUPS [450 G]

8 OZ [230 G] BEETS, PEELED AND HALVED

1 TBSP OLIVE OIL, PLUS MORE FOR GARNISH

½ TSP KOSHER SALT

8 OZ [230 G] GOAT CHEESE

2 TBSP MINCED SOFT HERBS (SUCH AS PARSLEY, CHIVES, DILL, AND MINT), FOR GARNISH

This (basically) two-ingredient dip is a tribute to the ubiquitous beet and goat cheese salads of the '90s. I'm looking at you, Wolfgang Puck. Because the goat cheese has so much tang and salt, and the beets are so sweet and earthy, these two ingredients barely need anything extra to shine—just a little bit of olive oil and salt for roasting the beets. Serve this with crudités or use it to make Endives with Beet Goat Cheese & Smoked Salmon (page 85). If you have leftovers, try this on a sandwich with roasted vegetables.

DIRECTIONS

Preheat the oven to 400°F [200°C].

In a small casserole dish, add the beets, olive oil, and salt. Use a spatula to toss and coat the beets. Cook for about 30 minutes, tossing every 10 minutes, until a fork easily pierces the beets. Let cool for about 10 minutes, or until the beets are slightly warm but not hot.

Transfer the beets to a blender or food processor with the goat cheese, and pulse for about 1 minute, until the mixture is smooth and creamy. This dip can be made ahead of time and stored in a sealed container in the refrigerator for up to 3 days. When you're ready to serve, transfer to a bowl, drizzle with olive oil, and garnish with the herbs.

MAKES 2 CUPS [160 G]

TOFFEE-TOASTED CORNFLAKES

2 CUPS [55 G] CORNFLAKES
1/4 CUP [55 G] UNSALTED BUTTER
1/4 CUP [50 G] PACKED LIGHT BROWN SUGAR
½ TSP KOSHER SALT

These crackly, buttery cornflakes take about 15 minutes to make and can add a touch of personality and texture to any dessert. Make a batch of these a few days before your party to sprinkle onto ice cream sundaes, chocolate pudding (like the Lightning-Fast Chocolate Pudding on page 150), or the Salty Peanut Butter Budino (page 154).

DIRECTIONS

Preheat the oven to 300°F [150°C]. Place the cornflakes in a medium mixing bowl, and line a sheet pan with parchment paper or a silicone baking mat.

In a small saucepan over medium-low heat, combine the butter and brown sugar. Once the butter is melted, cook for about 2 minutes, stirring once or twice, until the sugar has completely dissolved and the mixture is bubbling up the sides of the pan.

Pour the mixture over the cornflakes and toss to coat each flake. Sprinkle the salt in, stirring to evenly distribute it. Spread the cornflakes on the parchment paper–lined sheet pan, and bake for 8 to 10 minutes, stirring halfway through, until the cornflakes are lightly toasted. Let cool completely before breaking them into clusters. Transfer the clusters to an airtight container and store at room temperature for up to 3 days.

VANILLA SALT

MAKES ¼ CUP [70 G]

1 SPENT VANILLA BEAN
OR ½ UNUSED VANILLA BEAN, SPLIT LENGTHWISE

¼ CUP [70 G] FLAKY SALT (SUCH AS MALDON OR JACOBSEN)

The first time I made a batch of vanilla salt, it was to try a recipe from Renee Erickson's *A Boat, a Whale, and a Walrus*, which pairs the floral-sweet seasoning with fresh tomatoes and olive oil. Vanilla salt has since become one of my favorite ways to use spent vanilla beans. This technique captures the fresh aroma of the bean without any of the astringency or volatility of an alcohol-based extract that you might cook with. A ¼ cup batch will last for months and can add layers of luxury to both savory and sweet dishes (try it as a finishing salt for chocolate chip cookies or chocolate pudding).

DIRECTIONS

Break the vanilla bean into three or four small pieces. In a 6 to 8 oz [180 to 240 ml] airtight glass jar, combine the vanilla bean pieces with the salt. Seal the jar and shake vigorously to combine. For the best flavor, let the salt sit for a day or two before using. The salt can be stored at room temperature in this airtight jar for up to a year.

MAKES 1¾ CUPS [415 ML]

SOUR CHERRY SYRUP

1 CUP [200 G] SUGAR

1 CUP [140 G] SOUR CHERRIES, LEFT WHOLE

JUICE OF 4 LEMONS, ABOUT ¾ CUP [175 ML], STRAINED

In New York every summer, during the tiny sliver of July when you can find sour cherries at the farmers' market, I always grab a few pints. Their vivid red color and tart taste sets them apart from their sweeter counterparts, and while they practically beg to be baked into pies and coffee cakes, I prefer to drink them. I do this by making a quick, outstandingly pink syrup by simmering whole cherries (you don't even need to remove the pits or stems) with sugar, water, and lemon juice. I use this syrup in my Better-Than-Canned Cherry Cola (page 180), my Mini Sour Cherry Ice Cream Floats (page 163), and just mixed with seltzer for an absurdly easy nonalcoholic cocktail.

DIRECTIONS

In a small saucepan over low heat, combine all the ingredients with 1 cup [240 ml] of water. Simmer for 30 minutes. Remove from the heat and let cool to room temperature. Store the syrup and cherries together (the cherries will continue to color the syrup) in an airtight container in the refrigerator for up to a week. Strain before using the syrup (and try adding the cherries to oatmeal or yogurt).

SNACKS

Before

DINNER

ARRANGE A PLATTER • TOSS IN A BOWL

SNACKS *Before* DINNER

You know the common anxiety dream where you're back in school, taking an exam you didn't study for? For me, it's usually a dream where guests start knocking on my door, but I haven't started any of my dinner prep yet, and I have to break the news to them that there will be nothing to eat for hours. In reality, we've all probably been that host before—the one who underestimated how long it would take to clean the house, pick up groceries, and cook our way through a few recipes.

This chapter is all about the food you can set out the moment your doorbell rings, to buy yourself time to make cocktails, put the finishing touches on dinner, or turn your attention to the party snacks that you want to actually serve hot (more about those in the next chapter). Many of these recipes have elements that can be prepped a day or two in advance, requiring only a few minutes of assembly before serving, and all of them taste great at room temperature. Need a few minutes to check on something in the oven or babysit something on the stovetop? Just pour some Rosemary Brown Sugar Party Mix (PAGE 64) into a bowl and pull a plate of Pickled Mussel Gildas (PAGE 91) out of the fridge to keep everyone happy in the meantime.

For the smoothest sailing the day of your party, read through each recipe ahead of time so that you can have all the ingredients ready to go, and don't be afraid to supplement with bowls of olives, tins of fish (SEE PAGE 23 FOR SUGGESTIONS), and a big old loaf of bread on a cutting board.

ROSEMARY BROWN SUGAR PARTY MIX

MAKES 5 CUPS [300 G]

2 CUPS [60 G] CORN CHEX (OR CRISPIX)
1 CUP [60 G] PRETZEL STICKS
1 CUP [30 G] CORNFLAKES
1 CUP [120 G] PECANS
3 TBSP UNSALTED BUTTER
2 TBSP PACKED LIGHT BROWN SUGAR
2 TSP MINCED ROSEMARY
½ TSP KOSHER SALT
½ TSP PAPRIKA
¼ TSP GARLIC POWDER
¼ TSP ONION POWDER

This recipe falls somewhere between a store-bought snack mix and a batch of homemade bar nuts, and it's my dream combo of sweet, salty, crunchy, and nutty. The butter, brown sugar, rosemary, and pecans give the mix a toasty, cozy feel, and the blend of paprika, garlic powder, and onion powder adds a nostalgic grocery-store-snack-aisle kick. This mix will last for up to a week in an airtight container, which means that it's not just a great make-ahead option for gatherings, but also an easy gift to bring in a big jar to a friend's party.

DIRECTIONS

Preheat the oven to 350°F [180°C].

In a large mixing bowl, combine the Chex, pretzel sticks, cornflakes, and pecans.

In a small saucepan over medium heat, combine the butter, brown sugar, and rosemary. Cook for about 2 minutes, swirling frequently, until the mixture thickens and bubbles up. Pour it over the Chex mixture, and stir to coat. Sprinkle the salt and seasonings over the mixture, then stir to evenly distribute.

Spread the snack mix onto a sheet pan lined with parchment paper or a silicone baking mat. Bake for 15 minutes, stirring every 5 minutes. Allow the snack mix to cool completely before packing it into a tightly sealed container. Store at room temperature for up to 1 week.

SERVES 6 TO 8

HAM & HAZELNUTS

8 OZ [230 G] IBÉRICO HAM, SERRANO HAM, PROSCIUTTO, OR COPPA
½ CUP [70 G] SKINNED HAZELNUTS
1 TBSP UNSALTED BUTTER
½ TSP LEMON ZEST
LEMON WEDGE, FOR GARNISH

This combination is a tribute to the Ibérico ham and hazelnuts at Septime La Cave in Paris. The pairing is so simple but brilliant. I've seen it take off on wine bar menus around the world, and I'd like to make the case for enjoying it at home, too. Although you could make this anytime throughout the year and serve it with whatever drinks you like, it is an ideal fall accompaniment to a glass of red wine. Call me fussy, but I find that it's worth it to use skinned hazelnuts so that you don't get any of the mealy husk texture messing with the buttery combo of nuts and ham. Order these online, and you'll find yourself using up the rest rapidly, throwing them into batches of granola or crushing them over Dutch babies with a drizzle of maple syrup.

DIRECTIONS

Arrange the ham in a fanned-out formation on a platter or large dinner plate and allow it to come to room temperature and soften while you toast the hazelnuts.

In a small saucepan, add the hazelnuts and butter. Cook over low heat, swirling frequently, for about 5 minutes, until the butter has started to brown and the hazelnuts have turned light brown in spots. The whole mixture should smell nutty and toasted.

Spoon the buttered hazelnuts over the ham and finish with the lemon zest. Serve with a lemon wedge for squeezing over the top.

SERVES 4 TO 6

QUICK-MARINATED ANCHOVIES WITH KUMQUATS

1 SMALL GARLIC CLOVE (OR HALF OF A LARGE ONE), GRATED
2 TBSP GOOD-QUALITY OLIVE OIL
10 SALT-CURED, OIL-PACKED ANCHOVY FILLETS, DRAINED
3 KUMQUATS, THINLY SLICED AND SEEDED
1 SPRIG MINT, TORN INTO SMALL PIECES
¼ TSP PINK PEPPERCORNS, COARSELY GROUND

$15 plates of anchovies have become ubiquitous on restaurant menus in recent years. It's a dish that anyone could "make" at home in a few minutes, but restaurants count on the fact that most home cooks don't have a cache of quality anchovies. I'm here to tell you that you *can* (and should) have a stockpile of really good anchovies on hand. With a few kumquats, a clove of garlic, and good olive oil, you can turn those anchovies into a dish that would do numbers at your neighborhood wine bar. The flavors will continue to meld as the party goes on, leaving you with a plate of citrusy, garlic-scented olive oil for bread dipping when all the anchovies have been eaten. Seek out firm-fleshed anchovies from brands like Codesa, Don Bocarte, Fishwife, Sea Tales, Siesta, or Ortiz (Siesta and Ortiz both sell enormous round tins of anchovies that are perfect for parties). If you're having trouble tracking down kumquats, don't let that hold you back—just use a few very thin slices of lemon.

DIRECTIONS

On a serving plate (or a regular dinner plate), use a fork to gently whisk together the grated garlic and olive oil. Lay the anchovies across the plate's surface, in the olive oil. Scatter the kumquats, mint, and pink peppercorns on top and serve.

SERVES 4 TO 6

SALT & VINEGAR CHIPS WITH CRÈME FRAÎCHE & SMOKED TROUT ROE

8 OZ [230 G] CRÈME FRAÎCHE

1 OZ [30 G] SMOKED TROUT ROE

1 TSP MINCED CHIVES

ONE 7½ OZ [215 G] BAG OF STURDY SALT AND VINEGAR POTATO CHIPS (SUCH AS KETTLE OR CAPE COD)

I'm all for taking the time to caramelize a skillet of onions for a batch of onion dip or getting the blender out for a silky smooth hummus, but when guests are five minutes away, this three-ingredient snack delivers the drama. While most dips are designed for plain vessels—bread, crackers, plain chips—in this scenario, the salt and vinegar are important parts of the equation. Each bite of these acidic chips is cooled and tempered by the creamy, mild dairy and salty pops of fish eggs.

DIRECTIONS

Scoop the crème fraîche into a small bowl. Mound the trout roe on top and sprinkle the chives across the surface. Set the bowl in the center of a wide, shallow bowl and scatter the chips around it. Serve immediately.

CHIP

Tricks

TOWER THEM HIGH

A few years ago, Ernesto's, a Basque restaurant on the Lower East Side, started serving a mile-high tower of alternating layers of house-made potato chips and Ibérico ham. Since then, I've seen chip towers pop up on cooking websites, friends' Instagrams, and many more restaurant menus. To make your own, layer potato chips in a shallow bowl, alternating with layers of charcuterie, tinned mussels, or finely grated cheese.

MAKE SOME CHIP DUST

Crushed potato chips are a shortcut to texture, richness, and salt. I'm especially fond of crushed salt and vinegar chips when I want to add acidity and vinegar flavor to a dish without adding liquid. You can use crushed chips to garnish a dip, add breading to something you're frying (try them on chicken cutlets), or as a topping for a casserole.

MAKE A SHORTCUT SPANISH TORTILLA

Have some semi-stale chips left in the bag a few days after the party? Take a page from chef Ferran Adrià's 2011 book *The Family Meal*, and cook them into eggs for a quick and satisfying frittata or tortilla.

CANDIED MARCONA ALMONDS WITH CUMIN SEEDS & ORANGE ZEST

MAKES 2 CUPS [400 G]

½ CUP [100 G] SUGAR

4 TSP VEGETABLE OIL (OR ANOTHER NEUTRAL OIL WITH A HIGH SMOKE POINT)

2 CUPS [280 G] UNSALTED MARCONA ALMONDS

2 TSP CUMIN SEEDS

1 TSP PIMENT D'ESPELETTE (OR OTHER FINELY GROUND CHILI FLAKES)

1 TSP KOSHER SALT

2 TSP ORANGE ZEST

In a pinch, when you need to buy some extra time to finish making dinner or cutting crudités, a bowl of salted marcona almonds will do wonders to keep guests happy. These almonds also have a buttery, savory quality that makes them a great candidate for a little added spice. I like to give them a crackly coating of caramelized sugar and toss them in cumin seeds, chili, and orange zest. This trio of seasoning balances delicately between sweet and savory, creating a satisfying snack where each bite is a little bit different. Make a batch of these a few days ahead of time for a party, pack them as a hiking snack, or bring a jar of them to a friend as a host gift.

DIRECTIONS

Line a sheet pan with parchment paper or a silicone baking mat. In a large stainless-steel skillet or saucepan over medium heat, combine the sugar and oil. Cook for about 4 minutes, watching carefully and stirring constantly, until the sugar starts to melt. If the sugar starts to burn, turn the heat down to low.

Add the almonds and cumin seeds and cook, stirring constantly, for about 1 minute, until the almonds are lightly toasted and the sugar is clinging to them in a thick syrup.

Pour the almonds onto the prepared sheet pan. Sprinkle the piment d'Espelette, salt, and orange zest over the almonds while stirring to evenly distribute. Spread the almonds into a thin layer. Let cool completely. Break the almonds up into small clusters, and transfer them to a sealed container. Store at room temperature for up to 3 days.

NDUJA OYSTER CRACKERS

MAKES 2 CUPS [150 G]

2 TBSP UNSALTED BUTTER

16 SAGE LEAVES

2 TBSP NDUJA

2 TSP HONEY

2 CUPS [100 G] OYSTER CRACKERS

Because oyster crackers are so salty and dry, they're astoundingly good at absorbing nearby fats and flavors (this is probably why they're such a popular choice for sprinkling onto chowder or turning into ranch-flavored firecrackers). In this recipe, I pair them with nduja, a fully cooked, spreadable sausage that's full of rich, vivid red pork fat and spice. Nduja is a favorite fridge staple of mine to stir into pasta sauces and bowls of brothy beans, but here, it becomes the main character of a crunchy drinking snack, punctuated by bits of fried sage. It all comes together with about 5 minutes of stovetop stirring—you just fry some sage in butter, render the nduja into that butter, and bathe oyster crackers in it (with a little bit of honey to help everything stick).

DIRECTIONS

In a medium skillet over medium-low heat, melt the butter. Add the sage leaves, and cook, stirring frequently, for about 3 minutes, until they have stiffened and curled. Transfer the sage leaves to a small plate lined with a paper towel.

Turn the heat down to low, and add the nduja and honey to the pan, stirring and swirling to incorporate. Add the oyster crackers, and toast them, stirring and scraping the bottom of the skillet, for 2 minutes.

Remove the skillet from the heat. Set 5 or 6 sage leaves aside for garnish, and crumble the rest of the leaves into the oyster crackers, stirring to incorporate them. Transfer the crackers to a small serving bowl, and top with the remaining sage leaves.

MAPLE BUTTER SHICHIMI TOGARASHI POPCORN

MAKES ABOUT 12 CUPS [115 G]

2 TBSP VEGETABLE OIL (OR OTHER NEUTRAL OIL)
½ CUP [115 G] POPCORN KERNELS
2 TBSP UNSALTED BUTTER
1 TBSP MAPLE SYRUP
½ TSP TABLE SALT (OR OTHER FINELY GROUND SALT)
½ TSP SHICHIMI TOGARASHI
PINCH OF CITRIC ACID

Years ago, during a happy hour at Clyde Common in Portland, Oregon, I ordered a bowl of popcorn dusted with shichimi togarashi. This recipe is my ode to that bar snack, created after about a decade of dusting my popcorn with the Japanese spice blend and other ingredients with the goal of bringing out all its fruity, floral flavors. Shichimi togarashi typically contains sesame seeds, chili, orange peel, and nori. I pair it with a faintly maple-sweetened butter and the tiniest pinch of citric acid to bring out the flavor of the orange peel. If citric acid isn't already in your pantry, it should be—a jar will last you for years, and it will make all your popcorn seasoning blends and spice mixes taste better.

DIRECTIONS

Heat a medium saucepan over medium heat for about 1 minute, or until you can feel some heat emanating from the pan when you hold your hand a few inches above it. Add the oil and popcorn kernels. Cover, and cook, shaking lightly, until most of the kernels have popped and you start to hear several seconds of silence between pops.

In a small microwavable bowl or saucepan, melt the butter with the maple syrup. Transfer the popped popcorn to a large mixing bowl, leaving behind any unpopped kernels. Toss the popcorn with the butter, salt, shichimi togarashi, and citric acid. Serve immediately.

ESTATE

SERVES 4

APPLES & GOUDA DRIZZLED WITH HONEY & BLACK PEPPER

2 MEDIUM HONEYCRISP OR FIRESTORM APPLES, QUARTERED, CORED, AND CUT INTO THIN SLICES

4 OZ [115 G] AGED GOUDA, CUT INTO UNEVEN SHARDS ABOUT ¼ IN [6 MM] THICK

2 TSP HONEY

¼ TSP FRESHLY GROUND BLACK PEPPER

If you haven't noticed, a lot of the recipes in this book are basically glorified kid foods (okay, maybe not the tinned barnacles). This one is a classic after-school snack of apple slices and cheese cubes that's been spruced up with gouda, a drizzle of honey, and a sprinkle of black pepper. I love how this combination puts the spotlight on crunchy, juicy fall apples. Aged gouda is a firm cheese that's nutty and intensely savory, and it never gets enough attention when it's part of a cheeseboard. Beemster and Marieke Gouda are a few favorites, but there are many more to explore.

DIRECTIONS

On a serving plate, fan the apple slices so that the skin is visible, and arrange in a few clusters. Scatter the gouda around the apples, drizzle the honey over everything, and sprinkle with the black pepper. Serve immediately.

Snacks

MAKES 30 CANAPÉS

ENDIVES WITH BEET GOAT CHEESE & SMOKED SALMON

2 ENDIVES [280 G], TRIMMED AND PULLED APART INTO LEAVES

1 RECIPE BEET GOAT CHEESE (PAGE 54)

4 OZ [115 G] SMOKED SALMON, CUT OR TORN INTO BITE-SIZE PIECES

½ OZ [14 G] CHIVES, MINCED

Endives can truly do it all, which is why I always seem to have a few knocking around in my crisper drawer. They add crunch to salads, they help fill out platters of crudités, and their canoe-like shape makes them perfect for two-bite canapés. For this recipe, I pair endives with a sunny combination of Beet Goat Cheese (page 54) and smoked salmon. Some grocery stores will sell small end pieces of smoked salmon for a lower by-the-pound price, which are perfect for hors d'oeuvres like this. If you want to keep a few vegetarian-friendly, skip the salmon or swap it out for a few briny capers to garnish.

DIRECTIONS

Spread the endive leaves out on a platter and spoon about 1 teaspoon of the goat cheese onto the bottom end of each one (I like to keep this toward the root end so that the other end can be easily picked up). Set a piece of salmon on top of each spoonful of cheese and sprinkle the chives over each endive. Serve immediately.

MAKES 30 CANAPÉS

ENDIVES WITH WHITEFISH & TROUT ROE

2 ENDIVES [280 G], TRIMMED AND PULLED APART INTO LEAVES
8 OZ [230 G] WHITEFISH SALAD
1¾ OZ [50 G] TROUT ROE
½ OZ [14 G] CHIVES, MINCED

A few years ago, when I hosted a tinned fish tasting at Platform by the James Beard Foundation, the event space's culinary team turned the smoked trout dip from my book *Tin to Table* into beautiful passed hors d'oeuvres to serve as a welcome snack with sparkling wine. They simply spooned some of the smoky dip onto purple endives and topped each bite with chives and trout roe. The smoked trout dip continues to be one of my favorite recipes in *Tin to Table*, but this recipe swaps it out for whitefish salad, which you can pick up from the grocery store or your local bagel shop. Serve with champagne or cava.

DIRECTIONS

Spread the endive leaves out on a platter and spoon a teaspoon or two of the whitefish salad onto the bottom end of each one (I like to keep this toward the root end so that the other end can be easily picked up). Spoon a few pieces of trout roe onto each spoonful of whitefish, sprinkle a few chives on top of each, and serve.

SERVES 4 TO 6
FOR A SMALL BITE

TINNED BARNACLES WITH SMOKED PAPRIKA AIOLI

¼ CUP [60 G] SMOKED PAPRIKA AIOLI (PAGE 52)
ONE 4 TO 6 OZ [115 TO 170 G] TIN OF BARNACLES, DRAINED
1 LEMON WEDGE

If you've never encountered them before, gooseneck barnacles (or percebes) look a little like miniature dinosaur feet and taste like a luxurious cross between a crab and a mussel. These crustaceans are harvested at low tide from the surfaces of rocks and cliffs—a difficult task that makes them a pricy and prized delicacy. Because they have a short shelf life after they've been harvested, it's incredibly rare to find them for sale in fish markets and restaurants (I have only ever ordered them fresh at a restaurant once, at Traveling Mercies, in Denver). Luckily, canning preserves these barnacles' delicate, briny flavor and yields a texture that's even more tender and delicate than when they're prepared fresh. Tins of barnacles from brands like Wildfish Cannery, Conservas de Cambados, and Los Peperetes are not cheap, but they make stunning hors d'oeuvres—and are a great conversation starter.

DIRECTIONS

Put the aioli in a small cup on a small serving plate. Arrange the drained barnacles around it and squeeze the lemon wedge over them. Serve with a small bowl for the shells. (Canned barnacles are eaten like tail-on shrimp—picked up by the shell/foot, which is then discarded.)

MAKES 12 GILDAS

PICKLED MUSSEL GILDAS

12 PICKLED COCKTAIL ONIONS

ONE 4 OZ [115 G] TIN OF MUSSELS IN ESCABECHE (SUCH AS RAMÓN PEÑA, MATIZ, OR SIESTA CO. BRANDS)

12 CORNICHONS

Gildas, a salty Spanish drinking snack, usually take the form of an anchovy, an olive, and a piparra skewered together into one harmonious bite on a cocktail pick. This particular gilda celebrates the beauty of the tinned mussel. Tinned mussels in escabeche sauce (sometimes labeled as "mussels in pickled sauce" or "pickled mussels") are packed in a punchy orange marinade that combines olive oil, vinegar, garlic, paprika, and bay leaf. I always keep my pantry well stocked with these because they're one of the most sustainable species of seafood to buy, they're very nutritious, and they're beautifully prepared and ready to enjoy straight from the can. These gildas pack a vinegary punch with tinned mussels, cornichons, and cocktail onions. Pair them with something bitter and fizzy (like the Punt e Mes & Soda on page 175) and something rich (like the Cheese Dreams on page 109).

DIRECTIONS

Skewer a cocktail onion, a mussel, and a cornichon onto each cocktail pick. Serve immediately.

SNACKS *for* DINNER

MAIN EVENTS • HEARTY BITES

SNACKS *For* DINNER

Picture this: You're an hour into hosting a party. Your guests have already finished their first round of drinks and tried every flavor of potato chip, popcorn, and snack mix you've put out for them, and they're already starting to think about where to pick up a slice of pizza on the way home. It's time to pull out the big guns—the dinner snacks.

This chapter is about the warm skillets, savory tarts, and other heartier snacks that you could piece together into a meal, whether you're having a big, casual party or just a couple of friends over to watch a movie. Of course, you can serve these at any point, including before dinner, but if you're forgoing table settings and cutlery, these will provide an alternate way of feeding everyone with variety, color, and excitement. I've personally eaten the Confited Cherry Tomatoes (PAGE 99), Caesar Oeufs Mayonnaise with Chicories (PAGE 121), and Shrimp in Chili-Garlic Browned Butter (PAGE 125) with hunks of bread for dinner plenty of times.

Many of these recipes, like the Cheese Dreams (PAGE 109), Canned Clam Croquettes (PAGE 115), and French Onion Pie (PAGE 111), can be prepped ahead and frozen, giving you the option to cook and serve them whenever it feels right. That doesn't necessarily have to be when you're hosting—try a few Cheese Dreams alongside a bowl of tomato soup, or a few croquettes with a big salad for your next weeknight dinner.

MAKES 3 CUPS [710 ML]

WHIPPED FETA WITH BURNT HONEY

¼ CUP [85 G] HONEY
14 OZ [400 G] FETA, CRUMBLED
2 CUPS [480 G] PLAIN GREEK YOGURT (PREFERABLY FULL FAT)
1 GARLIC CLOVE, ROUGHLY CHOPPED
2 TSP OLIVE OIL
BLACK LAVA SALT OR FLAKY SALT, FOR FINISHING

There's something about the combination of salty, tangy feta and floral honey that works in flaky phyllo pastries, in savory galettes, or just baked together into a cozy appetizer to drag a piece of bread through. But my favorite way to enjoy this combination is in a cool, refreshing dip made by blending feta, plain yogurt, and a tiny bit of garlic. Because the feta already has so much acidity and salt, the dip barely needs any seasoning, but I like to garnish mine with a swirl of burnt honey—honey that's been caramelized over low heat until it darkens and thickens and takes on a slightly more savory characteristic. After a drizzle of olive oil and a sprinkle of salt, this dip is ready to serve with sugar snap peas, radishes, and grilled bread that's been brushed with olive oil and rubbed with a clove of garlic.

DIRECTIONS

In a small saucepan over low heat, cook the honey for about 10 minutes, until it bubbles up and starts to turn from a light golden color to a reddish amber color. Once this color change occurs, remove from the heat immediately, and stir in 2 tsp of water. Let the honey cool and thicken while you make the dip.

cont.

In a blender, add the feta, yogurt, and garlic. Pulse for a few seconds, then stop to scrape the sides of the blender before pulsing again. Pulse for a total of about 30 seconds, or until the visible chunks of feta have disappeared into the dip. (Be careful not to blend for too long, since this can damage the protein structure of the feta and make the whole mixture watery. If this happens, try gradually blending in more feta until you reach a thick, yogurt-like consistency.)

Spread the dip across the surface of a shallow bowl. Drizzle with the honey followed by the olive oil. Finish with salt and serve.

NOTE → If you overblend the feta and it becomes too liquidy (or if you just end up with leftovers), this dip doubles as an amazing marinade for chicken, penetrating the meat with briny, garlicky flavor. Just cover the chicken in the dip inside a large, covered bowl, and marinate it overnight before shaking off the excess and roasting.

SERVES 4 TO 6

CONFITED CHERRY TOMATOES

ONE 12 OZ [340 G] CARTON OF CHERRY TOMATOES
½ CUP [120 ML] OLIVE OIL
6 GARLIC CLOVES
1 TSP SUGAR
½ TSP KOSHER SALT
1 DRIED ARBOL CHILE
6 SPRIGS FRESH OREGANO
WARM, CRUSTY BREAD, FOR SERVING

Long before there were slow cookers and Instant Pots, there was confit—the hands-off method of slowly poaching a vegetable or a protein in olive oil, giving it a silky, rich texture and a flavor that can only be achieved with time and gentle heat. Confiting cherry tomatoes brings out their sweetness, infuses them with garlic, and transforms them into a jammy topping for bread. In this case, the skillet doubles as a serving dish that will keep your confit warm, but the confit tastes just as comforting at room temperature as it does fresh from the oven. If you wind up with leftovers (of the tomatoes or just the flavorful oil), save them in a jar in the refrigerator to toss with spaghetti.

DIRECTIONS

Preheat the oven to 250°F [120°C].

In a 6 in [15 cm] cast-iron skillet or 1 qt [1 L] casserole dish, gently toss together the cherry tomatoes, olive oil, garlic, sugar, salt, and chile.

cont.

The tomatoes should fit in one layer in the skillet or dish, with the olive oil covering them about halfway. Scatter the oregano sprigs around the skillet, and gently push them under the surface of the olive oil.

Cook for 1 hour, gently stirring the tomatoes halfway through to keep the tops from drying out or burning. Serve directly from the skillet or casserole dish, with a warm loaf of bread on the side. Store leftovers in an airtight container in the refrigerator for up to 1 week.

SCALE IT UP → If you're making this for a larger gathering, or if you want leftovers to toss with spaghetti the next day, double this recipe and use a 12 in [30.5 cm] cast-iron skillet or 2 qt [1.9 L] casserole dish.

VEGGIE Tricks

KEEP YOUR PREPPED VEGGIES MOIST

Cutting veggies ahead of time to serve with that bowl of dip? Gently wrap them in a damp paper towel before sealing them in a plastic container or ziplock bag and storing them in the refrigerator. This will help keep the veggies from drying out. I like to cut cucumbers at the very last minute to keep them crisp and juicy.

BRING THEM BACK FROM THE DEAD

If your pre-cut veggies are looking a little bit limp, or if you're cutting veggies a few hours before guests come over and don't want to pack them away in the fridge, set them in a bowl of ice water. This will keep everything crunchy and firm.

ALWAYS BLANCH WITH PLENTY OF SALT

If you're including vegetables like asparagus or green beans in your platter of crudités, you'll want to give them a quick blanch to tenderize them and bring out their sweetness. Generously salting the water will cook the vegetables faster, help lock in their bright green color, and make them taste better. Bring a pot of water with a few handfuls of salt to a roiling boil, cook the vegetables for 2 to 3 minutes, and then transfer them directly to an ice bath before draining and serving.

SERVES 8

TOMATOES WITH CHILI BUTTER & CRUNCHY SEED CONFETTI

¼ CUP [55 G] UNSALTED BUTTER
1 TSP FINE RED CHILI FLAKES (SUCH AS GOCHUGARU OR PUL BIBER)
1 TSP MAPLE SYRUP
1 TSP SHERRY VINEGAR
4 BEEFSTEAK TOMATOES, CUT INTO WEDGES
¼ CUP [35 G] CRUNCHY SEED CONFETTI (PAGE 51)

August and September might just be the laziest times of the year for entertaining. But without composing an elaborate salad or turning on the oven, you can still piece together a well-rounded, fresh-looking (and tasty) party menu. Finding good tomatoes (ideally purchased a few days before your party to give them some extra time to ripen on the countertop) is the key. Here, I top tomato wedges with a one-minute stovetop chili butter and a handful of Crunchy Seed Confetti (page 51) to add texture and some nutty, toasted sesame and caraway flavor.

DIRECTIONS

In a small saucepan over low heat, melt the butter until it begins to bubble, about 1 minute. Add the chili flakes, maple syrup, and sherry vinegar, vigorously swirling the pan a few times.

Arrange the tomato wedges on a wide platter. Drizzle the warm chili butter over the tomatoes, sprinkle the seeds across the top, and serve immediately.

SERVES 6 TO 8

FRIED DATES WITH BLUE CHEESE & PICKLED CELERY

2 TBSP OLIVE OIL

18 PITTED DATES

¼ TSP FLAKY SALT

6 OZ [170 G] BLUE CHEESE, BROKEN INTO UNEVEN SHARDS AND CRUMBLES

1 RECIPE PICKLED CELERY (PAGE 46)

While I love eating devils on horseback (a.k.a. bacon-wrapped dates) at parties, I rarely enjoy the fussy process of stuffing and wrapping the dates, timing their cooking perfectly to line up with the start of the party, and dealing with the smoky mess that happens when bacon grease and date sugar combine on the oven floor. By contrast, frying dates in olive oil is quick and hard to mess up, and the dates take on a crackly, savory quality that goes beautifully with cold, creamy blue cheese and crisp pickled celery.

DIRECTIONS

In a large skillet over medium heat, warm the olive oil. Add the dates and cook for about 3 minutes, stirring constantly, until the dates have softened and become wrinkly and crackly. Remove from the heat and sprinkle with the flaky salt.

Scatter the dates, blue cheese, and pickled celery across a serving platter and serve. Provide a cup of toothpicks so that guests can build their own perfect bite.

MAKES 24 HORS D'OEUVRES

CHEESE DREAMS (MINIATURE CHEDDAR TOASTS WITH CORNICHONS)

6 SLICES WHITE BREAD

2 CUPS [160 G] GRATED SHARP ORANGE CHEDDAR CHEESE

½ CUP [113 G] UNSALTED BUTTER, MELTED AND THEN COOLED TO ROOM TEMPERATURE

1 LARGE EGG

2 TBSP DIJON MUSTARD

2 TBSP WORCESTERSHIRE SAUCE

½ TSP FRESHLY GROUND BLACK PEPPER

½ TSP KOSHER SALT

CORNICHONS, FOR SERVING (OPTIONAL)

On Christmas Eve, when I was a kid, my family would pack into the station wagon to head through snowy western New York to my Aunt Dorris and Uncle Bill's house for lasagna, Jell-O salad, and Cheese Dreams. One of Dorris's specialties, the pillowy double-decker rectangles of white bread were crisp around the edges, melty in the middle, and gloriously orange (possibly with some help from Cheez Whiz). My version of these dainty one-bite hors d'oeuvres uses a more old-fashioned combo of egg, butter, sharp orange cheddar, and a little Dijon and Worcestershire sauce to amp up the cheesy flavors. I like to skewer each Cheese Dream on a toothpick with a cornichon—it looks darling and adds a much-needed burst of cold acidity to contrast with the toasted cheese.

cont.

DIRECTIONS

Preheat the oven to 400°F [200°C]. Spread out the slices of white bread on a cutting board or sheet pan to dry out slightly while you prepare the other ingredients. (If you remember to do this an hour or two before you get started, the slightly dried-out bread will be even easier to work with.) Line a sheet pan with parchment paper or a silicone baking mat.

In a medium mixing bowl, combine the cheese, butter, egg, mustard, Worcestershire sauce, pepper, and salt with a wooden spoon until thoroughly combined.

Cut the crusts off the bread, and reserve them for another use (see Note). Cut each slice of bread into 8 rectangles.

Using a knife or offset spatula, spread the cheese mixture across the top of one piece of bread, then top it with another piece. Spread more of the mixture on top of that piece of bread and down the sides of the sandwich, then transfer it to the parchment-lined sheet pan. Repeat with the remaining bread and cheese.

(At this point, if you want to freeze some or all of the cheese dreams to serve at a later time, just put the whole sheet pan in the freezer. After 1 hour, the individual pieces will be firm enough to transfer to a tightly sealed container to freeze for up to 1 month. When you're ready to serve them, you can bake from frozen.)

Bake the freshly made cheese dreams for 15 to 17 minutes, or until the corners start to brown slightly.

Serve on toothpicks with cornichons (if using), or with cornichons on the side.

NOTE → Dry out leftover bread crusts in a 300°F [150°C] oven for about 10 minutes and then pulse in a food processor or blender to turn into bread crumbs.

SERVES 8

FRENCH ONION PIE

2 TBSP OLIVE OIL
6 TBSP [85 G] UNSALTED BUTTER, PLUS MORE, MELTED, FOR BRUSHING
2 LB [910 G] YELLOW ONIONS, HALVED AND THINLY SLICED
1 TSP KOSHER SALT
2 TSP FRESH THYME LEAVES
1 TBSP BALSAMIC VINEGAR
1 CUP [240 G] SOUR CREAM
4 OZ [115 G] GRUYÈRE, SHREDDED
6 SHEETS PHYLLO DOUGH, DEFROSTED
CARAWAY OR POPPY SEEDS, FOR GARNISH (OPTIONAL)

Is it possible to improve upon onion dip—the timeless combination of caramelized onions and sour cream? Not really, but it *is* possible to stuff that dip inside a crust of flaky phyllo dough to turn it into a sliceable, shareable party appetizer. In this case, I spread the dip (amped up with some fresh thyme leaves and shredded Gruyère) into a disk shape in the center of a stack of phyllo sheets, wrap the whole thing up, brush it with butter, and bake it until it's golden brown. Since the pastry provides some insulation, the filling will stay warm even while your guests start to cut wedges for themselves. This dish has some of the appeal of baked Brie—a centerpiece of crackly pastry giving way to a melty, creamy inside—but you don't have to serve it with any accoutrements for dipping. This pie can stand alone on a cutting board at a cocktail party, or you could serve it for dinner alongside a big salad and dainty cups of soup.

cont.

DIRECTIONS

Preheat the oven to 400°F [200°C]. Line a sheet pan with parchment paper or a silicone baking mat.

In a large skillet over medium heat, combine the olive oil with 2 tablespoons of the butter. Add the onions and salt, and stir to coat in the fat. Cook, stirring every few minutes, for about 45 minutes, until the onions have browned, reduced in volume, and are starting to stick to the skillet.

Add the thyme leaves and balsamic vinegar, and cook for 2 minutes, scraping up any brown bits. Remove from the heat, and transfer the onions to a small mixing bowl.

In the meantime, melt the remaining ¼ cup [55 g] of butter in the microwave or a small saucepan over low heat.

Add the sour cream and Gruyère to the onions, and mix well. (The onion dip filling can be made ahead of time and refrigerated in a sealed container for up to 3 days.)

Lay a sheet of phyllo dough on the prepared sheet pan, and cover the remaining dough with a damp paper towel to prevent it from drying out. Brush the single sheet of phyllo dough with a layer of melted butter, then add another sheet on top of that one, rotating it about 30 degrees so that it lies diagonally across the original one. Brush the second sheet with melted butter, and continue adding the rest of the phyllo sheets, rotating each one slightly.

Spoon the caramelized onion mixture into the center of the phyllo, spreading it into a 9 in [25 cm] diameter circle. Gently wrap the loose ends of the phyllo over the disk of onion filling, and use a wide spatula to flip the whole thing over so that all the loose seams are on the bottom.

Brush the surface of the phyllo with the remaining butter, and sprinkle with caraway or poppy seeds (if using). Bake for 25 minutes, or until the surface is golden brown. Cool for 10 minutes before serving.

MAKES 24 CROQUETTES

CANNED CLAM CROQUETTES

3 TBSP UNSALTED BUTTER

1 CUP PLUS 2 TBSP [270 ML] OLIVE OIL

1 YELLOW ONION, DICED

1 CELERY STALK, DICED

1 TSP KOSHER SALT, PLUS MORE FOR SEASONING

¼ TSP BLACK PEPPER

¾ CUP [105 G] ALL-PURPOSE FLOUR

1½ CUPS [360 ML] WHOLE MILK

ONE 6½ OZ [185 G] CAN CHOPPED CLAMS IN THEIR BRINE

2 LARGE EGGS

1 CUP [60 G] PANKO BREAD CRUMBS

When done right, a Spanish-style croquette is a miracle of textures—a crackly brown crust that gives way to a lava of creamy béchamel. These savory snacks are often a resourceful way to use up the last few odd bits of Serrano ham left on a leg bone. My version features a slightly cheaper ingredient that you can find at most grocery stores: canned chopped clams. The béchamel is seasoned with lots of celery and onion, making each bite taste a little bit like a spoonful of clam chowder (no bowls or spoons required). Since these are fried and best served hot, some careful coordination is required to get them on the table at the right moment. To streamline the process, make and chill the béchamel and form the croquettes a few days before your party, and fry these up once your guests have arrived and are comfortably situated with a round of drinks.

cont.

DIRECTIONS

In a wide stainless-steel or nonstick skillet over medium heat, melt the butter with 2 tablespoons of the olive oil until the mixture is bubbling.

Add the onions, celery, salt, and pepper, and cook, stirring frequently, for about 3 minutes, until the vegetables have softened and turned translucent.

Add ½ cup [70 g] of the flour, and cook, stirring constantly, for about 2 minutes, until the flour has been completely mixed into the fat and has started to toast very slightly and turn a blond color.

Add the milk and the chopped clams with their brine, and cook for 3 to 5 minutes, stirring constantly, until the flour is evenly incorporated and the liquid has thickened into a paste. Remove from the heat and season with more salt and pepper if you'd like.

Allow the béchamel to cool to room temperature, then transfer it to the refrigerator in a covered container. Let cool for at least 2 hours, until the mixture is chilly to the touch and has a scoopable texture. You can expedite this process by cooling the béchamel in a wide, shallow dish, like a glass baking dish or ceramic casserole dish.

Using two metal soup spoons (or other large-ish spoons), form the béchamel into 24 oblong logs, each about 2 in [5 cm] long. Transfer each one to a parchment-lined sheet pan as you work. It's okay if the croquettes are a little bit lumpy and ugly at this point.

Stick the sheet pan in the freezer for 5 minutes while you set up your breading station. Prepare 3 small bowls by filling one with the remaining ¼ cup [35 g] of flour, one with the eggs, and one with the panko bread crumbs. Whisk the eggs until combined.

Use a pair of metal spoons to transfer each croquette first into the flour bowl to coat, then into the egg bowl, then into the panko bowl. Once a croquette has been coated in bread crumbs, use your hands to gently round it into a smooth oval shape, then return it to the parchment-lined sheet pan.

At this point, if you want to freeze the croquettes, you can transfer the sheet pan to the freezer for 1 hour to firm them up, then transfer the individual croquettes to a sealed container in the freezer for up to 2 months. If you're serving the croquettes sooner but aren't quite ready to fry them, you can cover the sheet pan and refrigerate it for up to 24 hours.

When you're ready to fry the croquettes, set a metal cooling rack over a sheet pan next to the stove, and heat the remaining 1 cup [240 ml] of olive oil in a small skillet or saucepan over medium-low heat (the olive oil should be at least ½ in [13 mm] deep but should not be close enough to the top of the skillet that it might spill over the sides).

You can test the oil's temperature by dropping a piece of panko into it. If the bread crumb is quickly surrounded by tiny bubbles, the oil is hot enough. Use a large metal spoon to carefully lower in a few croquettes at a time (they should not be touching one another), and fry them for about 5 minutes, carefully flipping each one halfway through. If you're starting with frozen croquettes, fry them for 6 minutes. As the croquettes finish cooking, transfer them to the prepared cooling rack, and sprinkle with salt. Serve hot.

SERVES 4 TO 6

NECTARINES WITH RICOTTA, OLIVE OIL & BLACK PEPPER

1 CUP [240 G] WHOLE-FAT RICOTTA

1 TSP OLIVE OIL

FRESHLY GROUND BLACK PEPPER AND FLAKY SALT, FOR FINISHING

3 RIPE NECTARINES, PITTED AND CUT INTO NARROW WEDGES

Whenever I have ricotta left over from a batch of lasagna or a baking project, it inevitably becomes a dip for whatever bread or bits of fresh fruits and vegetables I have lying around. I especially love the way the milky-fresh cheese tastes with perfectly ripe stone fruit. As powerful as this combo is as a cleaning-out-the-fridge desk snack during the workday, it's also a way to bring in-season fruit into a warm-weather dinner menu or party spread. A drizzle of olive oil and a sprinkle of salt and pepper tilts this slightly into savory territory, but it's still light and fresh enough to eat at any time of day (including brunch).

DIRECTIONS

Scoop the ricotta into a small bowl, using the spoon to make a small valley in the middle of the scoop. Drizzle the olive oil into the valley, and sprinkle with salt and pepper. Serve with a platter of nectarine slices.

Reserved
Enjoy

MAKES 12

CAESAR OEUFS MAYONNAISE WITH CHICORIES

6 LARGE EGGS

1 SMALL HEAD OF RADICCHIO OR PINK CASTELFRANCO, LEAVES SEPARATED

¾ CUP [180 G] CAESAR AIOLI (PAGE 53)

1 TBSP MINCED CHIVES

Oeufs mayonnaise is a classic French bistro staple that typically takes the form of an appetizer before dinner or a light lunch when combined with a baguette. When the dish is done right, it's a culmination of a perfectly cooked egg and a fluffy, well-seasoned mayo—almost a pared-down deviled egg. In recent years, chefs have reinvented the dish with caviar, truffles, squid ink, preserved lemon, yuzu kosho, and many more flourishes of personality. My own house oeufs are perched on cups of pink Castelfranco lettuce (or radicchio), which serves two functions: adding a refreshingly bitter crunch to complement the umami-packed mayo and making it easier and tidier for guests to scoop up an egg for themselves.

DIRECTIONS

Fill a medium pot with about 4 in [10 cm] of water, and bring it to a boil. Gently lower each egg into the water and set a timer for 8 minutes. In the meantime, prepare an ice bath in a medium mixing bowl. When the timer goes off, immediately transfer the eggs from the boiling water to the ice bath.

Arrange 12 of the chicory leaves on a platter, cupped side facing up. Peel the eggs and slice each one in half lengthwise. Place each half flat-side up on one of the chicory cups. Spoon about a tablespoon of the aioli onto each egg, and sprinkle with chives. Serve immediately.

MAKES APPROXIMATELY
1½ CUPS [450 G]

SHRIMP BUTTER & SALTINES

½ TSP KOSHER SALT, PLUS MORE FOR SHRIMP-COOKING WATER
8 OZ [230 G] SHRIMP, PEELED AND DEVEINED (SEE NOTE)
½ CUP [115 G] UNSALTED BUTTER
½ YELLOW ONION [2¾ OZ OR 80 G], MINCED
½ STALK CELERY [½ OZ OR 14 G], MINCED
¼ CUP [10 G] MINCED PARSLEY
½ TSP CAYENNE PEPPER
SALTINES, FOR SERVING
LEMON WEDGES, FOR SERVING

When I was growing up, my grandma Dorothy routinely made a shrimp mousse that consisted of canned shrimp, canned tomato soup, cream cheese, and gelatin, formed in a fish-shaped Jell-O mold. This wobbly monument to processed ingredients, served with stacks of saltines, was a staple at her parties, right alongside the glass bowl of sherbet punch. As a kid, I was always way too terrified to try it, but as an adult, I found myself looking for my own version of this retro dish to serve at parties. My prayers were answered when I came across a recipe in James Beard's *American Cookery* that combined softened butter with minced poached shrimp, onion, and parsley. I started to experiment with my own shrimp butters, adding some celery for crunch and a touch of cayenne for bite. I like to serve this with a knife for spreading, a stack of saltines, and a few lemon wedges.

cont.

DIRECTIONS

Bring a small pot of salted water to a boil. Add the shrimp, and cook for 3 to 4 minutes, or until they are opaque all the way through to their centers. Drain the shrimp, then transfer to a blender, food processor, or cutting board, and let cool until the shrimp are not too hot to handle.

If you're using a blender or food processor, pulse the shrimp a few times with the salt, butter, onion, celery, parsley, and cayenne pepper. If you're using a cutting board, mince the cooked shrimp, and fold it together with the other butter ingredients in a bowl.

Refrigerate in a sealed container for up to 3 days. Serve at room temperature, in a small crock or bowl, with saltines and lemon wedges.

NOTE → Seek out wild-caught domestic shrimp or farmed shrimp that's certified by an independent nonprofit like the Global Seafood Alliance or the Aquaculture Stewardship Council.

SERVES 6 TO 8

SHRIMP IN CHILI-GARLIC BROWNED BUTTER

¾ CUP [170 G] UNSALTED BUTTER

2 LB [910 G] SMALL, CLEANED SHRIMP, TAIL ON (SEE NOTE)

8 GARLIC CLOVES, MINCED

1 TBSP FINELY GROUND CHILI, SUCH AS PUL BIBER, GOCHUGARU, OR SILK CHILI

2 TSP KOSHER SALT

¼ CUP [10 G] MINCED PARSLEY

This shrimp falls somewhere between Spanish gambas al ajillo and Turkish tereyağlı karides—two dishes that involve a lot of shrimp, a lot of garlic, and a lot of flavorful fat left in the pan for dipping bread into. Because this takes all of 5 minutes of actual cooking time, this is a quick way to add a bit of sizzle to your snack spread. Serve with plenty of bread for dunking.

DIRECTIONS

In a large stainless-steel or carbon-steel skillet over medium heat, heat ½ cup [113 g] of the butter until it is melted and bubbling. Add the shrimp, and cook, stirring constantly, for 2 minutes, or until they have mostly turned pink and opaque but are still transparent in spots.

cont.

Add the garlic, chili, and salt, and cook for 1 minute, or until the shrimp is cooked through. Transfer the shrimp and the butter mixture to a small casserole dish or ceramic serving dish.

Add the remaining ¼ cup [55 g] of butter to the skillet and cook, stirring frequently to scrape up any remaining bits of garlic or spice, until the butter has bubbled up and begun to brown slightly (this will take 2 to 4 minutes, depending on how large the skillet is and how hot the burner is).

Drizzle the browned butter over the shrimp. Sprinkle the parsley over the top, and serve immediately.

NOTE → Seek out wild-caught domestic shrimp or farmed shrimp that's certified by an independent non-profit like the Global Seafood Alliance or the Aquaculture Stewardship Council.

MAKES 12 MINI SANDWICHES

SHRIMP BUTTER & CUCUMBER SANDWICHES ON BRIOCHE

6 SLICES BRIOCHE

1 RECIPE SHRIMP BUTTER (PAGE 123)

6 PERSIAN CUCUMBERS, THINLY SLICED LENGTHWISE

½ LEMON, FOR GARNISHING

These delicate little open-faced sandwiches turn the Shrimp Butter (page 123) into a composed snack that's fit for afternoon tea *or* 8:00 p.m. martinis. The sweet, crisp rectangles of brioche are a perfect match for the savory butter, which shields the bread from getting soggy under the weight of the refreshing, lemon-spritzed cucumber slices. If you prefer a closed sandwich, feel free to double the amount of toasted brioche, but personally, I like showing the cucumber slices tiled across the surface.

DIRECTIONS

Toast the brioche slices until they're stiff to the touch and lightly golden on each side. Cut off the crusts, and set aside for another use (such as bread crumbs, croutons, or stuffing).

Spread each slice of brioche with a generous layer of shrimp butter. Tile the cucumber slices across the surface, and squeeze the lemon over the top. Cut each of the open-faced sandwiches in half and serve.

SERVES 8 TO 10

MATRIMONIO TARTINE

ONE 20 IN [51 CM] BAGUETTE

1 RECIPE TOMATO CHILI BUTTER (PAGE 47)

TWO 2½ OZ [70 G] TINS SALT-CURED ANCHOVIES PACKED IN OLIVE OIL, DRAINED

4 OZ [115 G] BOQUERONES, DRAINED

½ OZ [14 G] CHIVES, MINCED

In Spain, the matrimonio pintxo typically pairs two contrasting preparations of anchovies. There are the deeply umami salt-cured anchovies, which are aged in salt-filled barrels before being cleaned and marinated in olive oil. And there are boquerones, which are silvery-white and pickled in vinegar (these can be found in the refrigerator section of some specialty grocery stores). This recipe turns a baguette, great anchovies, and some Tomato Chili Butter (page 47) into the red-and-silver striped centerpiece of the snack table. The Tomato Chili Butter adds a warmth and sweetness that complements the one-two punch of salty and briny anchovies. If you want to offer a fishy option and a vegetarian option, set aside half of the baguette and half of the butter to make the Pickled Pepper Tartine (page 133). Serve this on a big, cool cutting board with a bread knife.

DIRECTIONS

Cut the baguette in half lengthwise. Spread the tomato chili butter evenly across both halves. Cover the bread in the anchovies, alternating types. Sprinkle with the chives and serve.

SERVES 8 TO 10

PICKLED PEPPER TARTINE

ONE 20 IN BAGUETTE

1 RECIPE TOMATO CHILI BUTTER (PAGE 47)

2 OZ [55 G] ASSORTED PICKLED COCKTAIL ONIONS AND PEPPERS, SUCH AS PIPARRAS, BIQUINHOS, AND PEPPERONCINI, HALVED LENGTHWISE

½ OZ [14 G] CHIVES, MINCED

Much like the Matrimonio Tartine (page 131), this recipe pairs the caramelized, garlicky taste of the Tomato Chili Butter (page 47) with briny pickled peppers and cocktail onions. With a baguette, a make-ahead compound butter, and a few pantry jars, you'll have a rustic, colorful, satisfying tartine to cut into wedges or break off in chunks. I am always bringing home new types of pickled peppers from olive bars or the Bosnian grocery store in my neighborhood (you never know when you're going to need to spice up a tuna sandwich or charcuterie plate). For a cool visual effect and some exciting variation in each bite, I like to use a variety of shapes and sizes here, but if you only have piparras or pepperoncini, those will do the trick.

DIRECTIONS

Cut the baguette in half lengthwise. Spread the tomato chili butter evenly across both halves. Scatter the pickled peppers and cocktail onions across the surface. Sprinkle with the chives and serve.

PUFF PASTRY RICOTTA TART, THREE WAYS

SERVES 4 TO 6

15 OZ [425 G] RICOTTA

ZEST OF 1 LEMON

½ CUP [15 G] GRATED PARMESAN

½ TSP KOSHER SALT

¼ TSP FRESHLY GROUND BLACK PEPPER

ONE 17.3 OZ [490 G] PACKAGE FROZEN PUFF PASTRY, DEFROSTED

1 LARGE EGG, LIGHTLY BEATEN

Do you ever look at your party menu and wish you had something a bit heartier, or a few more hits of fresh produce? This tart does it all. It's a layer of flaky pastry, topped with creamy ricotta and fresh or lightly cooked fruits, vegetables, herbs, or alliums. The premise here is that if you have a package of frozen puff pastry in your freezer and a batch of this seasoned ricotta in your refrigerator, you can make a savory tart with whatever's in your crisper drawer. Have leftover roasted squash, or too many caramelized onions, or some beautiful fresh apricots, or nice anchovies? Turn them into a tart to cut into rectangles for party guests or to eat for dinner alongside a cup of soup. If you want to bring more color and variety to your party, you can even turn one package of puff pastry into two different kinds of tarts. This dish is good at room temperature, but it's best while warm, so pull it straight out of the oven and onto a big wooden cutting board for serving.

DIRECTIONS

Preheat the oven to 400°F [200°C]. Line one or two sheet pans (depending on whether the puff pastry comes in one big sheet or two small sheets) with parchment paper or silicone baking mats.

In a small bowl, mix together the ricotta, lemon zest, Parmesan, salt, and pepper. (This can be made ahead of time and refrigerated in a sealed container for up to 3 days.)

Spread the puff pastry out on the sheet pan. Use a knife to make a border, about ½ in [13 mm] around the edge of the pastry sheet, cutting about halfway down into the pastry, but not all the way through. Use the knife to pierce a few holes around the middle of the pastry, to prevent bubbling.

Brush the border of the pastry with the egg, using the knife to gently re-score the border if any of the egg wash drips into the crease. Bake for 5 minutes.

Spread the ricotta mixture across the surface of the puff pastry, staying within the pre-cut border. Add the toppings of your choice (see pages 138 and 139 for suggestions), then return the pastry to the oven for another 20 to 30 minutes, or until the edges are golden brown and puffed up and the bottom of the pastry is brown but not burned.

cont.

MUSHROOM BALSAMIC TART

2 TBSP OLIVE OIL

1 LB [455 G] BABY BELLA (CREMINI) MUSHROOMS, THINLY SLICED

½ TSP KOSHER SALT

½ TSP FRESHLY GROUND BLACK PEPPER

4 GARLIC CLOVES, MINCED

2 TSP BALSAMIC VINEGAR

1 SPRIG PARSLEY, LEAVES PICKED

DIRECTIONS

In a medium skillet over medium heat, heat the olive oil. Add the mushrooms, salt, and pepper. Cook, stirring frequently, for 10 to 12 minutes, until the mushrooms have released their liquid, shrunk, and started to brown around the edges. Add the garlic and cook, stirring frequently, for 1 minute. Add the balsamic vinegar and cook, stirring frequently, for 1 minute, or until it has reduced and there is no liquid pooling in the skillet.

Scatter the mushrooms across the surface of the ricotta. After baking the tart, garnish it with the fresh parsley leaves.

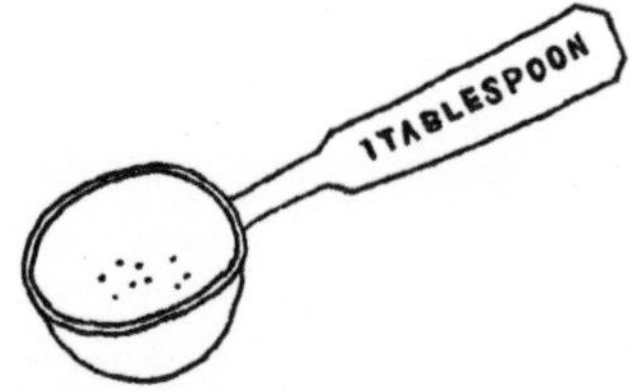

PEACH & RED ONION TART

1 SMALL RED ONION, HALVED AND THINLY SLICED INTO HALF-MOONS
1 YELLOW PEACH, PITTED AND CUT INTO THIN SLICES
2 TSP OLIVE OIL
1 TSP FRESH THYME LEAVES
⅛ TSP FLAKY SALT

DIRECTIONS

Lay the onion and peach slices in an alternating pattern across the surface of the ricotta. Brush with the olive oil, and sprinkle with the thyme and salt.

ASPARAGUS, SCALLION & CAPER TART

4 SCALLIONS, THINLY SLICED
2 TBSP CAPERS, DRAINED
8 OZ [230 G] ASPARAGUS, WOODY ENDS TRIMMED AND THINLY SLICED LENGTHWISE
2 TSP OLIVE OIL

DIRECTIONS

Sprinkle the scallions and capers across the surface of the ricotta. Lay the asparagus slices across the top in stripes. Brush with the olive oil.

Sweets

FANCY FINISHERS • SOMETHING FRUITY

SWEETS

I strongly believe that even the most casual parties deserve a dessert course. Even if it's totally phoned in—an open box of Italian bakery cookies in the center of the table and a few bottles of amaro and scotch pulled out of the liquor cabinet—the gesture puts a perfect cap on the evening while keeping the party going just a little longer. If you're catering to a group with a range of dietary restrictions, maybe dessert is simply a bowl of clementines or Cantaloupe with Vanilla Salt (PAGE 147) and a plate of good dark chocolate bars broken into sample-size pieces.

But if you have time the week before entertaining to put some thought into dessert, the possibilities get even more exciting. You can make a batch of Lightning-Fast Chocolate Pudding (**PAGE 150**) and a batch of Salty Peanut Butter Budino with Toffee-Toasted Cornflakes (**PAGE 154**), and turn them into swirly little parfaits for each guest. Or you can freeze a loaf pan of Plum Granita (**PAGE 157**) to serve with or without whipped cream and caramel sauce for a vegan-friendly palate cleanser.

If you have freezer space for a gallon of ice cream and plenty of serving bowls or glasses, an array of quick desserts becomes possible. Microwave a batch of Pistachio Magic Shell (**PAGE 165**) to pour over the top, scoop the ice cream into Mini Sour Cherry Ice Cream Floats (**PAGE 163**), or add a splash of Fernet and a sprinkle of espresso grounds for the Fireplace Gelato (**PAGE 145**).

SERVES 1

FIREPLACE GELATO (CHOCOLATE ICE CREAM, ESPRESSO POWDER & FERNET)

2 OZ [55 G] CHOCOLATE GELATO
1 TSP FERNET-BRANCA
¼ TSP FINELY GROUND ESPRESSO

Who needs espresso martinis when you can just serve your ice cream with a splash of Fernet and a sprinkle of espresso powder? This dessert was inspired by Marcella Hazan's Chimney Sweep's Gelato, from *Essentials of Classic Italian Cooking*, which combines vanilla gelato, espresso powder, and scotch. When I wrote about Hazan's recipe a few years ago for *Epicurious*, where I was an editor, I learned that the combination of flavors works together in an unexpected way. The alcohol and coffee create toasty top notes, and the cool, creamy gelato tamps down the bitterness of both. My twist uses chocolate gelato and Fernet-Branca. Fernet can be polarizing, but I like to keep a bottle around for digestifs and occasional cocktails. It has an herbal, mentholated quality that reminds me of a more subtle version of the crème de menthe that my grandma Dorothy used to serve over ice cream in dainty glass bowls.

DIRECTIONS

Scoop the chocolate gelato into a small dessert bowl or coupe glass. Pour the Fernet over the top and sprinkle the espresso across the surface. Serve immediately.

SERVES 4 TO 6

CANTALOUPE WITH VANILLA SALT

1 RIPE CANTALOUPE OR 3 RIPE SUGAR CUBE MELONS

½ TSP VANILLA SALT (PAGE 56)

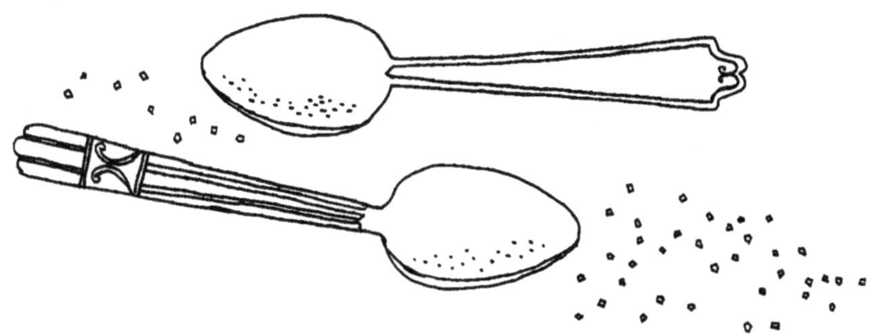

Although there are myriad sweet and savory ways to use vanilla salt and loads of baking applications, I find myself getting the jar out most often in late summer, when cantaloupe (and their softball-size counterparts, sugar cube melons) are in season. The pairing is low-maintenance, unexpected, and it cranks the summery flavors of the melon up to 11. This works as a refreshing snack before dinner, a brunch course, or breezy dessert.

DIRECTIONS

Cut the melon in half, and scoop the seeds out with a spoon. Cut each half into wedges 1 in [2.5 cm] thick. Arrange the wedges on a platter, and sprinkle them with the vanilla salt. Serve immediately.

SERVES 4 TO 6

PEARS & STILTON

2 BARTLETT PEARS, CHILLED, QUARTERED, CORED, AND THINLY SLICED
4 OZ [115 G] STILTON, ROOM TEMPERATURE

For as long as I can remember, my family has had a winter tradition of sitting around the table after a big dinner (after any children have deserted the scene) and passing around a big hunk of Stilton and a plate of sliced pears. The two contrasting ingredients combine into a complex, satisfying bite, ideally accompanied by a tiny glass of port. A stinky blue cheese might sound like a strange way to end a meal, but like the French tradition of saving the cheese course for last, it means that you can fully appreciate how rich and assertive that cheese is, without overpowering your palate for the rest of the meal. Really ripe, juicy, cold Bartlett pears are key here to create a refreshingly sweet foil to the cheese. For the creamiest cheese texture, pull the Stilton out of the refrigerator about an hour before serving.

DIRECTIONS

Fan the pear slices out on a plate. Serve the Stilton on a separate plate, with a cheese knife.

LIGHTNING-FAST CHOCOLATE PUDDING WITH COCOA CRUNCH

SERVES 6 TO 8

PUDDING

⅓ CUP [65 G] SUGAR

¼ CUP [20 G] NATURAL OR DUTCH PROCESS COCOA POWDER

2 TBSP CORNSTARCH

½ TSP KOSHER SALT

2 CUPS [475 ML] MILK (SEE NOTE)

5 OZ [140 G] DARK CHOCOLATE, ROUGHLY CHOPPED, OR 1 CUP [180 G] CHOCOLATE CHIPS (I LIKE 60% TO 70% CACAO)

½ TSP VANILLA EXTRACT

COCOA CRUNCH

¼ CUP [55 G] UNSALTED BUTTER, MELTED

¼ CUP [50 G] SUGAR

½ CUP [70 G] ALL-PURPOSE FLOUR

¼ CUP [20 G] NATURAL OR DUTCH PROCESS COCOA POWDER

1 TSP KOSHER SALT

My ideal chocolate pudding is light on the sugar, heavy on the salt and vanilla, and easy enough to throw together during a commercial break when the craving hits. For expediency, this one skips the whole process of tempering eggs. This recipe draws some inspiration from the chocolate pudding at Clown Bar in Paris, which is light and silky, served in a wide, shallow bowl, and sprinkled with little crunchy bits of chocolate streusel.

DIRECTIONS

TO MAKE THE PUDDING: In a medium saucepan, whisk together the sugar, cocoa powder, cornstarch, and salt. Add a splash of the milk and whisk into a paste (this will prevent clumps of the cornstarch from turning gummy and hard when the pudding cooks). Whisk in the rest of the milk, then turn the heat to medium.

Cook the mixture, whisking constantly, for about 5 minutes, until it starts to bubble and thicken. Continue cooking and whisking for 1 to 2 minutes, until the mixture coats the back of a wooden spoon. Remove from the heat, and gently stir in the chocolate and vanilla. Let sit for about 1 minute, until the chocolate has melted, and then stir to fully incorporate the chocolate and vanilla (at this stage, it's important to avoid whisking vigroursly, which can break the starch structure and result in a soupy texture). Serve warm, or transfer to an airtight container and refrigerate until ready to serve.

TO MAKE THE COCOA CRUNCH: Preheat the oven to 350°F [180°C] and line a sheet pan with parchment paper or a silicone baking mat. In a small bowl, mix together all the ingredients until they stick together in little clumps. Spread these out on the sheet pan, and bake for 10 minutes, stirring gently halfway through. Let cool completely before serving or storing in an airtight container at room temperature for up to 1 week.

TO SERVE: Divide the pudding among 6 to 8 small bowls or coupes, and top with a few spoonfuls of the cocoa crunch.

NOTE → I like the richness of whole milk, but you can also use a lower percentage or a plant-based milk.

SALTY PEANUT BUTTER BUDINO WITH TOFFEE-TOASTED CORNFLAKES

SERVES 8

1 LARGE EGG

2 LARGE EGG YOLKS

3 TBSP CORNSTARCH

⅔ CUP [130 G] PACKED LIGHT BROWN SUGAR

1½ TSP KOSHER SALT

2½ CUPS [600 ML] WHOLE MILK

1¼ CUPS [300 ML] HEAVY CREAM

½ CUP [170 G] UNSWEETENED OR LIGHTLY SWEETENED SMOOTH PEANUT BUTTER (SEE NOTE)

1 TSP VANILLA EXTRACT

1 RECIPE TOFFEE-TOASTED CORNFLAKES (PAGE 55)

WHIPPED CREAM OR CHOPPED TOASTED PEANUTS, FOR SERVING (OPTIONAL)

This cool, creamy custard is for my fellow Reese's obsessives. While budino is typically flavored with butterscotch or caramel, this one has a baseline sweetness from caramelized brown sugar, complemented by a good amount of peanut butter. I like to top each dish with a small handful of Toffee-Toasted Cornflakes (page 55), but you can get more elaborate with the toppings if you want, adding a dollop of whipped cream or a sprinkle of chopped peanuts. To prevent the sweetness from getting out of control, I like to use an unsweetened creamy peanut butter, like Once Again or Smucker's.

DIRECTIONS

In a small bowl, whisk together the egg, egg yolks, and cornstarch. Set aside.

In a medium saucepan over medium heat, combine the brown sugar, salt, and ⅓ cup [80 ml] of water. Cook for 8 to 10 minutes, until the sugar is dark, syrupy, and bubbling up the sides of the pot. You should notice the smell transform from a mild molasses scent to a caramelized sugar scent.

Add the milk, cream, and peanut butter, and bring to a simmer, whisking to evenly distribute the peanut butter. Once the liquid is simmering, carefully pour 1 cup [240 ml] of it into the egg and cornstarch mixture, whisking vigorously to keep the eggs smooth.

Add the tempered egg mixture back into the saucepan, and whisk for 3 to 5 minutes, until the liquid starts to thicken. Continue cooking and whisking constantly until the liquid is thick enough to coat the back of a wooden spoon. Remove from the heat.

Pour the custard through a fine-mesh sieve into a heatproof bowl. Stir in the vanilla, and let cool to room temperature.

If you have plenty of space in your refrigerator, portion the budino out into 8 glasses, ramekins, or sundae dishes, then cover and chill for at least 4 hours. If you're tight on space, refrigerate the budino for up to 3 days in one large, covered container, and spoon it into the individual bowls right before serving. Garnish with the toffee-toasted cornflakes and whipped cream and chopped peanuts (if using).

NOTE → For a sesame-forward version, substitute tahini for the peanut butter.

SERVES 8 TO 10

PLUM GRANITA WITH WHIPPED CREAM & SALTED CARAMEL SAUCE

GRANITA

1 LB [455 G] RIPE PLUMS (SEE NOTE), HALVED AND PITTED

¾ CUP [150 G] SUGAR

JUICE OF 2 LEMONS

SALTED CARAMEL SAUCE

⅔ CUP [130 G] SUGAR

½ TSP KOSHER SALT

1 CUP [240 ML] HEAVY CREAM

WHIPPED CREAM

1 CUP [240 ML] HEAVY CREAM

With their velvety jewel tones and understated sweetness, plums are about as glamorous as it gets. Throughout early autumn, I find myself simmering batches of plum jam to swirl into yogurt, bake into Marian Burros's famous plum torte recipe, and turn into this icy, creamy dessert. If you've never made a granita, it's as simple as freezing a sweetened purée and periodically scraping the ice crystals off the surface with a fork to keep the texture light and airy. The effect is a little like a sorbet, but you don't need an ice cream maker to make it. Like the fanciest restaurant desserts, this one requires some planning and artful assembly, but each element (granita, whipped cream, and caramel) can be made ahead of time, with only a handful of ingredients.

cont.

DIRECTIONS

TO MAKE THE GRANITA: In a blender, combine the plums, sugar, lemon juice, and 1 cup [240 ml] of water. Blend on high speed for 1 minute, or until the fruit has liquified and no large pieces of the skin remain intact.

Transfer the mixture to a medium saucepan. Simmer over medium-low heat for 10 minutes. Remove from the heat and let cool to room temperature. Pour the mixture into a metal loaf pan, and freeze it for 3 hours, using a fork to scrape up ice crystals every 30 to 40 minutes. Once the granita has fully frozen into fluffy ice and no longer has a slushy consistency, transfer it to a container with an airtight lid (to prevent freezer smells from making their way in).

TO MAKE THE SALTED CARAMEL SAUCE: In a small saucepan over medium heat, combine the sugar with 2 Tbsp of water. Cook for 5 to 7 minutes, swirling the pan occasionally, until the sugar has melted and turned an amber color. Carefully add the salt and heavy cream (it will sputter when it comes in contact with the molten sugar), and whisk over low heat for about 5 minutes, until the caramel has dissolved into the cream and thickened into a sauce. Remove from the heat and let cool to room temperature. This can be made up to 3 days in advance and stored in a sealed container in the refrigerator.

TO MAKE THE WHIPPED CREAM: With a whisk or a hand mixer, whip the cream until it's airy and about doubled in volume. Cover and refrigerate (ideally for less than 24 hours so that the cream doesn't deflate) until you're ready to serve.

TO SERVE THE GRANITA: Chill a set of glass coupes or short, squat bodega glasses if you have space in your freezer. Fill each glass about halfway with the plum granita, and top with a generous spoonful of whipped cream and about 1 Tbsp of caramel sauce. Serve immediately.

NOTE → Red-flesh sugar plums will give you the most vibrant color, but yellow plums or Italian plums also work.

MAKES 24 COOKIES

FREEZER RESERVE PISTACHIO-SESAME CHOCOLATE CHIP COOKIES

2 CUPS [280 G] ALL-PURPOSE FLOUR
1 TSP BAKING SODA
1 TSP KOSHER SALT
1 CUP [226 G] UNSALTED BUTTER, ROOM TEMPERATURE
1 CUP [200 G] PACKED LIGHT BROWN SUGAR
½ CUP [100 G] GRANULATED SUGAR
1 TSP VANILLA EXTRACT
2 LARGE EGGS
12 OZ [340 G] DARK CHOCOLATE (60% TO 70% CACAO), CHOPPED
1 CUP [140 G] TOASTED, SALTED PISTACHIOS, CHOPPED
¼ CUP [35 G] BLACK SESAME SEEDS

When I was in college and living in a dorm room with a shared kitchen, I got in the habit of making chocolate chip cookie dough a few times per semester and freezing the dough in ready-to-bake balls. This meant that when friends came over to study or listen to MP3s on terrible laptop speakers, I could always rustle up some warm cookies. A few decades later, I still do this. When my husband and I are watching a movie, or when friends stop over for a nightcap after dinner out, the freezer reserve has us covered. These cookies can be baked directly from frozen, making them an easy party trick you can pull out of the oven at just the right moment. I roll each ball of cookie dough in chopped pistachios and black sesame seeds to give the exterior a nutty, crunchy quality.

cont.

DIRECTIONS

Line a sheet pan with parchment paper or a silicone baking mat. In a small bowl, whisk together the flour, baking soda, and salt.

In a medium bowl, cream together the butter and both sugars. Stir in the vanilla and eggs until thoroughly combined, then stir in the dry ingredients until fully incorporated. Fold in the chocolate.

Form the cookie dough into 24 balls, and set them on the prepared sheet pan. Place it in the freezer for 10 minutes to firm up the dough.

In a small bowl, combine the pistachios and sesame seeds. Remove the dough from the freezer. Smooth the surface of each ball by rolling it between your hands briefly, then roll each ball in the pistachios and sesame seeds, returning them to the sheet pan once coated.

Return the sheet pan to the freezer. After 1 hour, the cookie dough balls will be firm enough for you to transfer them to a tightly sealed container or ziplock bag. You can store them in the freezer for up to 3 months.

To serve, preheat the oven to 350°F [180°C]. Arrange your desired number of cookies on a parchment-lined sheet pan, spacing them out by at least 2 in [5 cm]. Bake for 15 to 18 minutes, until the tops and edges are lightly browned. Let cool for 5 minutes before serving in order to firm them up slightly.

MAKES 1 FLOAT

MINI SOUR CHERRY ICE CREAM FLOATS

4 OZ [120 ML] SELTZER, CHILLED

2 TBSP SOUR CHERRY SYRUP (PAGE 57)

2 OZ [55 G] (ABOUT HALF A STANDARD SCOOP) VANILLA ICE CREAM

FRESH SOUR CHERRIES WITH STEMS ATTACHED, FOR GARNISH (OPTIONAL)

While I would love to be the kind of person who whips up a few sour cherry pies to serve with ice cream after a July dinner party, I usually find myself spending those last few pre-party hours running out for last-minute groceries, cleaning the bathroom, or trying to cool down the kitchen. These ice cream floats channel all that fruity summer flavor in a blissfully low-maintenance way. This recipe makes one float, but once you have the supplies, you can scale up easily. Just make a batch of Sour Cherry Syrup (page 57) a few days ahead of time, and keep a bottle of seltzer in the fridge and a pint of good vanilla ice cream in the freezer. Gather your daintiest jars or juice glasses, arrange them on a tray, and your own personal soda shop is in business.

DIRECTIONS

In an 8 oz [240 ml] jar or juice glass, add the seltzer and cherry syrup. Scoop the ice cream into the glass, and garnish with one or two fresh cherries (if using). Serve with a short metal straw.

SCALE IT UP → One full batch of the Sour Cherry Syrup (page 57) will make about 14 ice cream floats. If you're making this many floats, buy 2 L of seltzer (you'll use about 56 oz [1.7 L]) and 2 pints of ice cream (you'll use 28 oz [800 g]).

SERVES 4

PISTACHIO MAGIC SHELL

¼ CUP [65 G] PISTACHIO CREAM (I LIKE TO USE A CRUNCHY TYPE FOR THIS)

4 TSP COCONUT OIL

PINCH OF KOSHER SALT

ICE CREAM, FOR SERVING

Every time I see a new brand of pistachio cream, I compulsively add it to my shopping basket. The sweet spread is usually made by emulsifying toasted Sicilian pistachios with sugar, oil, and sometimes milk solids to give it a rich texture that's a little like Skippy peanut butter. I like using it to tint whipped cream a pale green, give pistachio flavor to lattes, and sweeten my oatmeal in the morning. My biggest pistachio breakthrough, however, was realizing that I could melt this cream with a little bit of coconut oil to give it a pourable texture to cloak a scoop of ice cream. Try this with vanilla or cherry ice cream, and if you want even more nutty flavor and crunch, top each scoop with a few crushed pistachios.

DIRECTIONS

In a small glass jar or measuring cup, combine the pistachio cream, coconut oil, and salt, and microwave for 30 seconds. Whisk everything together until you get a smooth, heavy cream consistency. Serve immediately over ice cream, using a heaping tablespoon of the topping for each scoop of ice cream. If you wind up with extra magic shell, you can store it in the refrigerator for up to 3 days in an airtight jar. Just microwave for 30 seconds and whisk again when you're ready to use it.

SCALE IT UP → If you're making this for a dozen or so friends, use 1 cup [260 g] pistachio cream, 5 Tbsp [70 g] coconut oil, and ¼ tsp kosher salt.

Drinks

FUZZY & REFRESHING • BALANCED & BITTER

DRINKS

These days, "cocktail party" is usually code for whatever-bottle-of-wine-everyone-shows-up-with party. That's probably a good thing. No one wants to wait in a cocktail bar–length line for drinks at their friend's house. If you have a few open wine bottles on your countertop, everyone can help themselves without disrupting conversation. For nondrinkers, there are more options than ever for fancy canned and bottled sodas and mocktails, from brands like Casamara Club, Ghia, and St. Agrestis.

But if you have time to make a homemade syrup, shrub, iced tea, or batched cocktail, or if you have a group small enough to take individual drink orders, this extra little gesture can show your guests that you've thought through every detail. I like to follow some timeless advice from James Beard's *Hors d'Oeuvre and Canapés*, which is to offer a maximum of two different cocktails at any given party. To further simplify things, I usually only serve cocktails at the front end of the party, before shifting to wine or beer.

If you don't want the pressure of standing around all night making drinks, you can set out a station with glasses, ice, seltzer, pre-peeled lemon twists, and a few mix-ins, like Sour Cherry Syrup (PAGE 57) and Sungold Vanilla Shrub (PAGE 182), as well as some vermouth to make the Punt e Mes & Soda (PAGE 175).

PIPARRA MARTINI

MAKES 1 MARTINI

2½ OZ [75 ML] GIN OR VODKA
½ OZ [15 ML] FINO SHERRY
½ OZ [15 ML] PIPARRA BRINE
1 PIPARRA, FOR GARNISH

I'm enthralled by piparras, the spindly green pickled peppers that are part of so many Spanish gildas and other pintxos. I am always finding ways to add them to sandwiches, pickle plates, and one-bite hors d'oeuvres. But their dainty proportions and delicate taste (like a more reserved, mature pepperoncini) also make them a beautiful cocktail garnish. I've had fantastic piparra martinis at both Txikito and the now-closed Huertas in Manhattan, and I love the way the salt and heat of the pepper contrasts with the ice-cold blend of gin (or sometimes vodka) and vermouth. My version follows classic martini proportions, swapping in some clean, dry fino sherry in place of the vermouth. The sherry swap, along with a splash of piparra brine, helps this martini lean in a savory (and supremely refreshing) direction.

DIRECTIONS

Place a coupe, Nick and Nora, or martini glass in the freezer to chill.

Add the gin, sherry, and piparra brine to a cocktail mixing glass (or a sturdy jar) with a handful of ice cubes. Using a cocktail spoon, stir vigorously for 30 seconds, or until the outside of the glass feels extremely cold.

Strain into the chilled glass, garnish with the piparra, and serve.

SCALE IT UP → If you're making this for a couple of friends, you can easily stir two drinks at a time in one mixing glass by doubling the amounts above. If you're making it for a larger group, consider batching and freezing a few hours before your party. To pre-batch 8 cocktails, mix 20 oz [600 ml] of gin, 4 oz [120 ml] of sherry, 4 oz [120 ml] of brine, and 4 oz [120 ml] of water in a plastic 1 qt [945 ml] container or glass jar. The water will make up for the dilution that you would otherwise achieve by stirring the drink with ice. Freeze for at least 4 hours before serving.

PICKLED CELERY GIBSON

MAKES 1 COCKTAIL

2½ OZ [75 ML] GIN
½ OZ [15 ML] DRY VERMOUTH
½ OZ [15 ML] BRINE FROM PICKLED CELERY (PAGE 46)
1 SMALL HANDFUL OF CELERY LEAVES (OPTIONAL)
1 PIECE PICKLED CELERY (PAGE 46), FOR GARNISH

Traditionally, a Gibson is a savory twist on a martini, substituting a cocktail onion for the olive. My version, which incorporates the very easy homemade Pickled Celery (page 46), has the same clean, briny qualities as the classic but with a touch of complexity from the pickling spices and a bright, leafy flavor. I like to stir my Gibson with a handful of celery leaves to amp up that fresh flavor, but if your celery is leafless, or if you're making this for a big group, feel free to exclude that ingredient. Serve a round of these at the beginning of a wintry cocktail party with a plate of warm, toasty Cheese Dreams (page 109).

DIRECTIONS

Place a coupe, Nick and Nora, or martini glass in the freezer to chill.

Add the gin, vermouth, brine, and celery leaves (if using) to a cocktail mixing glass (or a sturdy jar) with a handful of ice cubes. Using a cocktail spoon, stir vigorously for 30 seconds, or until the outside of the glass feels extremely cold.

Strain into the chilled glass, garnish with a piece of pickled celery on a cocktail pick, and serve.

MAKES 1 COCKTAIL

PUNT E MES & SODA

4 OZ [120 ML] PUNT E MES
4 OZ [120 ML] SODA WATER
LEMON TWIST, FOR GARNISH

Falling somewhere between the effort of pouring a glass of wine and making a full-fledged cocktail is the vermouth and soda. Because of vermouth's nuanced botanical notes, this two-ingredient drink punches way above its weight. It's bitter and bubbly and just what you need when snacking on oil-packed anchovies or Cantaloupe with Vanilla Salt (page 147). Whenever I can find it, I seek out Punt e Mes to keep in the fridge for these occasions. It's slightly more bitter than your average sweet vermouth, so it adds some spine to Manhattans, negronis, and quick sodas.

DIRECTIONS

Fill a rocks glass with ice. Add the Punt e Mes and soda water. Garnish with the lemon twist and serve.

ICE

Tricks

HELP! I FORGOT TO CHILL THE WINE

If a guest shows up with a room-temperature bottle of bubbly, or your fridge was too packed to chill wine ahead of time, an ice bath will get the job done fast. Just fill a big bowl about halfway with water, stirring in a few big handfuls of kosher salt. Submerge the bottles of wine and fill the rest of the space in the bowl with ice. In about 15 minutes, your drinks will be chilled.

POUR YOUR MARTINI INTO A FREEZING COLD GLASS

If you're only making a couple martinis, stick the glasses in the freezer while you're measuring ingredients and stirring the drink. If you're making martinis for a larger group or you don't have the freezer space to spare, borrow a trick from bartenders: Fill the glasses with ice water while you stir up the batch.

CLEAR ICE, FULL HEARTS, CAN'T LOSE

If you want to get *really* fancy with your cocktails, try making your own clear ice. Brands like ClearlyFrozen and Wintersmiths make ice cube trays that use directional freezing (freezing the liquid from the top down) to create completely transparent cubes that are free from air bubbles and clouds. *The Ice Book* by Camper English is a great resource for DIY ice projects that will make your cocktails more professional and more impressive.

NO RETORNABLE

BETTER-THAN-CANNED CHERRY COLA

MAKES 2 SERVINGS

4 OZ [120 ML] SOUR CHERRY SYRUP (PAGE 57)

ONE 12 OZ [ABOUT 360 ML] BOTTLE OF COLA (I PREFER TO USE SOMETHING WITH CANE SUGAR RATHER THAN CORN SYRUP, LIKE MEXICAN COKE)

2 SOUR CHERRIES, FOR GARNISH (OPTIONAL)

Cherry cola always sounds better to me in theory than it actually tastes whenever I make an impulse purchase (about every five years or so). It's usually way sweeter than I want it to be, and it can have almost a cherry ChapStick aftertaste. This is why, a few summers ago, I got in the habit of making a very tart Sour Cherry Syrup (page 57) to combine with bottles of Mexican Coke. Layered in a Collins glass, this cherry cola has all the drama of a tequila sunrise with none of the tequila (although you could always add some rum or fino sherry to turn this into a cocktail—1½ oz [45 ml] per glass will do the trick).

DIRECTIONS

Fill two Collins glasses with ice. Add 2 oz [60 ml] of the syrup to each glass. Divide the cola between the glasses, garnish each glass with a cherry, and serve.

MAKES 4½ CUPS [1 L]

MINT & MAPLE ICED TEA

4 BLACK TEA BAGS

1 BUNCH [40 G] FRESH SPEARMINT

¼ CUP [60 ML] MAPLE SYRUP

JUICE OF 2 LEMONS, PLUS 1 LEMON, SLICED, FOR GARNISH

Iced tea is massively underrated as a party beverage. It's hydrating, it's gentle on the stomach after a big meal, and when done right, it can be invigorating. This recipe takes inspiration from the iced tea I like to buy from the Wood Homestead Maple stand at the Grand Army Plaza greenmarket in Brooklyn. My formula is a little bit concentrated on purpose, so that even after it's been sitting in a pitcher full of ice (or an insulated tumbler full of ice at the beach) for a few hours, the flavors are balanced and crisp instead of watery.

DIRECTIONS

Boil 4 cups [945 ml] of water. Meanwhile, to a 1 qt [945 ml] glass measuring cup or medium mixing bowl, add the tea bags and half of the spearmint. Pour the boiling water over the tea bags and mint, and steep for 4 minutes.

Strain the tea into a 2 qt [1.9 L] pitcher, and mix in the maple syrup and lemon juice. Let cool to room temperature, then refrigerate the tea for at least 2 hours (or up to 3 days).

To serve, fill the remaining space in the pitcher with ice, lemon slices, and the remaining fresh spearmint. Alternatively, pour the tea into glasses filled with ice and garnishes.

SUNGOLD VANILLA SHRUB

MAKES 1½ CUPS [360 ML]

1 CUP [180 G] HALVED SUNGOLD TOMATOES (ABOUT 16 TOMATOES), PLUS MORE FOR GARNISH

1 CUP [240 ML] WHITE WINE VINEGAR

⅔ CUP [130 G] SUGAR

1 TSP VANILLA SALT (PAGE 56)

¼ TSP FENNEL SEEDS

½ TSP FRESHLY GROUND BLACK PEPPER

SELTZER, FOR SERVING

Shrubs are like a cheat code for making cocktails. These syrups, made from cooking together vinegar, sugar, and fruit, are a package deal—they bring sweetness, spice, vibrance, and acidity to a drink with every little spoonful. When I'm feeling too lazy to make my own (or uninspired by the ingredients in my kitchen), I love to mix seltzer with the drinking vinegars that Lindera Farms makes, which are flavored with ingredients like pawpaw, persimmons, and pine cones. But really, as long as you have vinegar and sugar in your pantry, plus one or two other ingredients to keep things interesting, you're only a few minutes away from a DIY batch. This shrub celebrates the sweet side of Sungolds and the savory side of vanilla. Mixed with seltzer, this shrub makes a sunny nonalcoholic cocktail in seconds flat—but feel free to add an ounce or two of mezcal or gin.

DIRECTIONS

In a medium saucepan over medium-low heat, combine all the ingredients. Cook for about 10 minutes, until the liquid is syrupy and the tomatoes have softened and lost their shape slightly.

Strain the mixture through a fine-mesh sieve, using the back of a spoon to push the tomato juice and pulp through. Cool to room temperature, then store in a sealed glass container in the refrigerator for up to 1 month.

To serve, combine 1 Tbsp of the shrub with 4 oz [120 ml] of seltzer over ice, and garnish with a few Sungolds on a cocktail pick.

ACKNOWLEDGMENTS

It's not a party without the people, and I couldn't have pulled off this party without the help of a wide cast of characters. Thank you to LINDA XIAO, MAEVE SHERIDAN, BARRETT WASHBURNE, ALEXIS GAMBLIN, ASHLEIGH SARBONE, CHRISTINA ZHANG, and CHARLOTTE FARMER for bringing the visuals in this book to life and making every single radish and cornichon shine.

Thank you to the book's designer, LIZZIE VAUGHAN, for always having a strong vision, a strong font, and a strong graphic pattern at the ready. Thank you to my editor, CLAIRE GILHULY, for ushering this book from an idea into a full-fledged piece of writing. Thank you to everyone else at CHRONICLE BOOKS who made this work possible. Thank you to my agent, ANGELA MILLER. Thank you to DAN BALL for eating so much puff pastry.

INDEX

D

E

F

G

H

I

K

L

M

N

O

P

R

S

T

V

W

Anna Hezel is the author of *Tin to Table: Fancy, Snacky Recipes for Tin-thusiasts and A-fish-ionados* and *Lasagna: A Baked Pasta Cookbook*. Her work has been featured in *TASTE, The New York Times, Bon Appétit, GQ, Rolling Stone, The Wall Street Journal, Eater, Food52, Lucky Peach*, and more. She lives in Brooklyn, New York.

EL COTO